In the image...
of a creative God

Dialogue, storytelling and creativity
through various media
to better communicate
the Good News of the Messiah
with the people of the Middle East

Richard J Fairhead

Published 2010, by 4cats Media, Larnaka, Cyprus

Richard Fairhead can be contacted through the website http://intheimage.info

---

Publishers Cataloging-in-Publication Data

Fairhead, Richard J, 1957-
In the image... of a creative God: Dialogue, storytelling and creativity through various media to better communicate the Good News of the Messiah with the people of the Middle East / Richard J Fairhead
120 p. 21 cm.
ISBN 1-4499-1113-7 (pbk.)
ISBN-13 978-1-4499-1113-3
1. Christianity and other religions -- Islam. 2. Creative ability -- Religious aspects -- Christianity. 3. Storytelling - Religious aspects - Christianity 4. Christianity -- Relations -- Islam.
(4cats Media)
BP 172
261 Fai

ISBN-10 1-4499-1113-7
ISBN-13 978-1-4499-1113-3

Typeset in Trebuchet MS

Contents

If you are a Muslim reading this book...

The book deals with the relationship between people who call themselves Christians and people who call themselves Muslims in the Middle East. As such I realise that this is a very sensitive subject. People have strong views about it. It's easy to take sides and think of 'us' and 'them'.

I share many things with Muslims: You and I both believe in one God, Allah. You and I both believe He created the heavens and the earth. You and I both believe that mankind does wrong, that we sin, and that we have never met someone who does not sin. You and I both want to please God. We both have a hope for something better after we die.

Surprisingly too, you and I both have problems with the organised church, with structural Christianity. If you asked me '*Are you a Christian?*' I might answer, '*Well, my mother and father were both Christians and I grew up a Christian. I respected them for what they believed, but now I would call myself a follower of Isa [or Jesus]*'. Another way I might express it, using Sufi language, is '*Mourideen el Massih*' - a follower or disciple of the Messiah.

This book contains four different sections. To start with I look at how Isa communicated what He believed. He was an excellent communicator and we should follow His ways. Then I look at the church and the different ways people see the church and how people become part of the church. I don't agree with all the models. I quote them to let people reading the book see the different ways that others see it. Personally I like the orientation and relationship models. In fact in the west I would call myself a 'relational Christian', I believe Isa spent much of His time on earth sitting and talking and sharing with people. The only people He came against were the religious rulers of His time who wanted to impose strict rules and regulations on the people.

The next section is for people who are trying to communicate using media between Christians and Muslims. Westerners love to measure things. Even though these scales are in the book, I am not sure how valuable they are. How can you measure love? How can you measure friendship?

That really is the centre of what I believe and why I want to see the way we communicate improved. I believe that God wants to have a relationship with us, to be our friend. I know for many Muslims this is a very strange idea, since I know from talking to you that they believe God is distant and far off. I agree that this is how He appears. But I know from personal experience that His desire is to be intimate with us and to show us how to intimately love Him. My desire is that Christians and Muslims can sit and share coffee and talk and listen to each other, to communicate. In that communication I believe we can learn from each other and that we will come to see the truth about God.

The final section is about creativity. I believe we are created in the image of God and that His creativity is imparted into us.

Introduction

For many years I have been involved with trying to share the Good News of Jesus Christ with people: young people through the youth groups at various churches, and others through media in the UK. More recently it has been through media in the Middle East and, of course, directly with the occasional person I might talk to about Jesus: everywhere from a transatlantic air flight to a meeting in the street.

I don't think I do it well. Looking around, I'm not sure many of us do it very well.

Some people I know are much more open and will talk about Jesus with almost everyone they meet... even with a stray customer coming out of the same restaurant in a same lift or elevator. But it's not how often we share Jesus that matters so much as whether we really do communicate.

When we try to explain who Jesus is to Muslims, it's pretty hard. And most of us feel we don't do that at all well.

I started writing this book as a result of attempting to develop methods for evaluating what we are doing in our media communication of the love of God to Muslims. The following methods were developed by a Muslim Background Believer with whom I shared my thoughts. In the process we became friends.

For some time the group I am involved with had been longing for a set of tools to help us evaluate what we do. Someone from another group worked with us for about six months, trying to get his head around the problem. He wrote, we talked, he thought. He talked with Arabs and he tried different methods, but it just didn't 'come together'.

However, something in the chemistry of having this friend from that background in our office every day for six to eight weeks worked, and we ended up with something we have found helpful. One of our aims, as a group, is to act as a catalyst for sharing the Gospel with Muslims through media. My colleague Peter said this should not just stay with us, but be shared further with others trying to do the same thing. So I started to write a book.

As soon as I started I realised that I wanted something out of it myself. Even if it never gets published my desire is that it will accomplish the second aim. That is, to help me think through the issues relating to communicating Christ in a post-modern Muslim context. I added the word post-modern because I think it's relevant for two reasons.

People have talked about this being a hinge generation, passing through from one established world view to another. Though the implications are very different in East and West I think something similar is happening all over the world.

As I see some post-modern attributes in the youth of the Middle East, I also see examples of pre-modern thought among the older generation there. There are two results of this: Firstly, there is a major culture gap between generations in the Middle East. Indeed, I would see the difference between a young person in the Middle East and their parents as being similar to the difference between a young person in the West and their great-grandparents.

Secondly, there is another significant culture gap when Western modernists attempt to communicate Christ to a simultaneously pre-modern and post-modern Middle East. It is as if people from the West attempt to sail through the gap between the two world views, without really making contact.

Much is written about post-modernism in a Western context, but almost nothing is being written from the point of view of the Middle East. So this book is a journey for me to research, and think through, and see what new things God is doing in the region. God is, as He always has been, creatively dealing with the world. We need to catch some of that creativity in communicating Jesus. This is a journey that can particularly influence the way we communicate the Good News to people from the Middle East.

There has been talk of an 'online church' linking believers from the Middle East together in secret. We have been working towards building online communities who have decided to follow Jesus. However, despite many reservations about the institutionalised church, I am not sure how the body of Christ can be anything other than incarnational. We are commended to meet together, and an online community lacks much that we gain from face-to-face communication and physically shared worship.

There is a third aim in writing this book for me, and that is to re-discover my place in the Body of Christ.

Recently I have become somewhat disillusioned with traditional evangelical church structures and communication techniques, tiring of its output of modernist verbiage. Though I am comfortable sharing the Good News about Jesus, I am not sure that the church is very good news for me, let alone the average Muslim.

Philip Yancey shares a similar path, though his disillusionment and re-finding happened when he was younger. GK Chesterton and CS Lewis were the two authors who he felt helped him along the path.

> *Although separated from me by a vast expanse of sea and culture, they kindled hope that somewhere Christians existed who loosed rather than restrained their minds, who combined sophisticated taste with a humility that did not demean others, and above all, who experienced life with God as a source of joy and not repression.*[1]

In answer to the question *Why did I return?* Yancey explains:

> *My career as a journalist gave me the opportunity to investigate people... who demonstrate that a connection with God can enlarge, rather than shrink, life. I began the lifelong process of separating church from God. Though I emerged from childhood churches badly damaged, as I began to scrutinise Jesus through the critical eyes of a journalist, I saw the qualities that so upset me – self-righteousness, racism, provincialism, hypocrisy – Jesus himself fought against, and that they were probably the very qualities that led to his crucifixion.*[2]

If we are to communicate the love of God to the people of the Middle East, we will need to find ways to separate their preconceived ideas (some of them painfully true) of the 'Christian message' we communicate, from the person who is both our and their Messiah.

While you are reading this, you will find that there are areas I leave open to discussion or debate. Sometimes those are in places where I cannot personally see a clear Scriptural direction. Other times, I do see a clear Scriptural direction, but know of other Biblical followers of Jesus who see things differently. One of the major differences between following Jesus and being a Muslim is the acceptance of diversity. We should celebrate this. It's part of our freedom in Christ. He treats us as people with whom He wants a relationship.

Post-modern Christians frequently object to didactic - formal, structured, unidirectional teaching. They do not talk about a set of doctrines, but about a dialogue. This book, then, is an attempt to start such a dialogue.

Richard J Fairhead
Autumn 2007

1 Soul Survivor - Philip Yancey - page 41
2 Soul Survivor - Philip Yancey - page 42-43

Acknowledgements

Although much of the content in this book had been on my heart and mind for some years, this book would never have been written if it were not for a group of YWAM leaders who run an English/Arabic Discipleship Training School in Cyprus with whom I have had a long and encouraging relationship. They were the people who met with, encouraged and taught the MBB [Muslim Background Believer] who spent time with us. Without them not only would I have never met this MBB, but he would not have had the background and knowledge to help me in this book. To them I owe a debt of gratitude.

Peter, my colleague, spent many hours and days talking through the various concepts and ideas and has commented on the final text. The Bible says how with many minds there is wisdom. Peter brings that to this project.

Paul was someone I got to know while on a visit to Australia. When discussing the project we discussed the similarities and differences of his context and ministry. Paul then went through the text with a fine tooth comb. As an editor he was invaluable, understanding the content and questioning where the text was unclear.

Joan also proof read the text and helped with style in a few places. She pointed out some of the problems with punctuation between American and British English. For the record, I am using British *open punctuation* which has a lot less marks than American. *Richard J Fairhead* is correct for modern British English. If you want a further insight into my thinking about spelling and punctuation please read the dialogue between author and publisher in the preface to *Seven Pillars of Wisdom* by TE Lawrence.

My family have endured this project, argued, debated, corrected and toiled to correct my English to make it comprehensible to anyone who thinks more logicaly than I ever do.

Most of all, this book would never have been possible were it not for God orchestrating that series of events and meetings that led to a Muslim Background Believer spending time with us. Some of the people who were His channels in this series of events I know, some I have heard of, and some I will never meet before we meet in Heaven. But more significantly, without God, I would have not been inspired to believe that everyone in the world should have the opportunity to get to know Him and enjoy a relationship with Him.

The "J" on the cover really bothers me because it has no period after it. Since there are differences between British and American English, maybe it would help to put an explanation in the Intro and then you are covered for those differences that look incorrect to us silly Americans.
JOAN

Contributors

Throughout this book you will see in the margins comments from various people who read and participated in the dialogue of this book. In places their comments reinforce what I wrote, in other places they bring context and in others they show the diversity of opinion within the Body of Christ. I have used their initials rather than their full names as some live and work in the Middle East and would find it difficult if their comments were used out of context in that region. Below is a brief description of each of the contributors:

PTR: Peter is involved with the same group I am and helps me lead that group. He has been involved with running Discipleship Training Courses for combined groups of Westerners and Middle Easterners. He plays guitar and occasionally leads people in singing praises to our Lord. He used to work for British Telecom Research Department the technical side, involved with media streaming on the Internet. He is married with three children.

MAX: Max is a follower of Jesus who comes from a Muslim background. He helped us develop the scales we now use. He is a creative writer and accountant, hence the understanding and the dealing with numbers. Without his help this book would have been impossible. I encourage you to pray for him, and for the millions like him who have yet to hear about the Messiah in a way that they can respond to, as your read through this book.

DAN: Daniel is my oldest son. He was home-educated, spent a year working as an actor and then four years sharing the love of Jesus with people around the world with a group of over 300 young people travelling together. Daniel and I used to love spending late nights talking about life, the world and the universe and in particular how God relates to the world we live in.

When I was far away from the Messiah I found that Christians are not open and not happy to talk about their religion – they are happy to preach at people but not open to dialogue.

I was calling people to follow my religion before I decided to follow Jesus and when I tried to invite a Christian to my faith I challenged him with 'Why do you think like a European when you have lived among Muslims for so long? I feel that Europe doesn't understand Islam, they just attack Islam. You should correct your ideas about Islam now you live among Muslims'.

I was expressing my feeling that Christians don't listen to Muslims. I think this is the key that if Christians really listened to Muslims then I don't think that the Muslims would convert the Christians to Islam, but that the Muslims would return to following the Messiah.
MAX

Creativity and dialogue

Jesus was a communicator. A storyteller. A teacher. We might have even called Him a media professional if He were alive today. He sometimes used the journalistic approach of asking the questions: who, what, when, how, where and why. And He loved dialogue. When He taught he was not afraid of interruptions. Indeed, He frequently used them to His advantage.

When we consider the character of the three personalities of the Trinity, we sometimes associate the creation of the world with Jesus. For instance, at the start of John's narrative we read that through Jesus, God made all things and nothing in creation was made without Him. However, the Apostles' creed sees the Father as the Creator of heaven and earth. Moreover, at the start of the Bible, the second sentence shows the Holy Spirit hovering or brooding over the waters. So all persons of the Trinity were involved in creation.

We often tend to see God the Father as primarily demonstrating holiness, compassion and righteousness. To the Holy Spirit we attribute the character of being the comforter, and the one from whom the fruits of love, kindness, gentleness and so on originate. However, many people find it easier to relate to Jesus; in Him, we see love, creativity, reconciliation and intercession.

Jesus said at one point that He would build a gathering of His people (often translated as 'church') and that even the gates of Hell would not be victorious against it[1]. Matthew's narrative of Jesus' life ends with Jesus commissioning His disciples to be His representatives: to go out and make more followers, adding to the gathering[2]. This gathering is now a world-wide group of His followers, who are learning about and following Him.

That commission, which is often taken as referring to all His followers from the early disciples onwards, is almost an echo of his personal call to two of the inner circle who were with Him for the three years that He communicated God's message on earth. James and John were fishermen, and Jesus called them to be 'fishers of men'[3].

When we think of fishermen, we sometimes think of those

1 Matthew 16
2 Matthew 28
3 Matthew 4

who fish for sport. People sit on the side of a river with a rod and line, casting out and reeling in the fish, one after another. But Jesus was talking about working fishermen: men with nets who cast them out, and bring in a whole haul of fish. If we are to bring in large hauls of people in the 21st century we need to use media as the nets. This, then, is the purpose of this book: to explore how we should use dialogue and creativity in media in our communication of the Gospel, and in our gatherings as the Body of Christ.

There are various theoretical models for how people become followers of Jesus or - if you prefer - members of His church. We have looked at these, and have incorporated one that came from someone who spent many years of his life sharing Jesus with people in the Middle East. His model echoed strongly the theology we see in John's Gospel: that the direction someone is heading is at least as significant as their position. Are they heading towards or away from the light?

However, we didn't feel that one person's direction told the whole story. So we combined two models, to create a new model that we believe is the most helpful in evaluating media for use in reaching and discipling people from the majority population of the Middle East.

As media professionals, we also looked at communication theory, to see how our belief in creativity and dialogue fitted in with that. We saw that a feedback loop is essential for effective communication, to ensure the accuracy of message delivery, and to allow for questions and clarifications. A feedback loop is what we might broadly call dialogue.

We have refined and developed our theoretical model. We added two scales that correlated with those created by people studying how we share the Gospel in a cross-cultural setting. We also added one that we developed ourselves. We wanted these scales not to evaluate people, but to help evaluate media. They helped us to see how appropriate – or otherwise – were the tools which we and others had created for different groups of people, at different stages of their walk towards or with the Lord.

The second of the scales is about what is called contextualisation. Contextualisation is a long word to describe the process of allowing the Gospel to be expressed within a culture. When we communicate, we inevitably use words which have meaning for us, but can frequently end up being meaningless jargon to the hearer. Or - worse – they could communicate something we specifically did not intend. For instance, a young man I know from a Buddhist background was told, when interested in knowing more about Jesus, that he needed to be 'born again'. He understood this as meaning that when he died, he would be re-incarnated.

So we need to think carefully about the words we use, and the way we communicate.

Assuming we are communicating in some way with someone who is listening, and theoretically interested in our message, there are three possible broad reactions. Someone could accept our message, reject it, or simply be bored by it. In a sense, allowing boredom is the worst reaction possible. It means that the person has not had an opportunity to interact with the content of the message. One cure for boredom is creativity. When we were created in the image of God, part of His nature to be creative was embedded into our nature. I believe we need to rediscover that, and find more creative ways of communicating His truth.

Jesus said that He is the way, the truth and the life. It is in the context of communicating His truth that we, as messengers of the Good News, labour. Our desire, our passion, our target, our goal if you like, is to bring people into an ongoing personal relationship with God our Father, and to work with Jesus and the Holy Spirit to build the gathering of His family among people from a Muslim background.

Jesus as a communicator

If we want to learn about communication, Jesus is probably the best teacher we could have to follow. Not only did He use multiple methods and techniques, He also modified His message to fit the culture or context of His audience. Moreover, He very effectively used dialogue at times as a feedback path, to ensure that His hearers understood what He was saying.

This chapter looks at three aspects of Jesus as a communicator: in dialogue with people, as a story-teller, and as a teacher. This is inevitably a snapshot; a whole book could be written about this subject alone. The aim of this chapter is partly to see a Biblical basis for what we are developing as a method. It is also to see examples of God's creativity in action. We are His followers, and we learn from Jesus as our Master.

Jesus in dialogue

Consider the following examples of His interaction with three different people: Nicodemus, a woman He met at a well in Samaria and the woman who was caught in the act of adultery.

Nicodemus[1]

Nicodemus was a pharisee, and a member of the Jewish council. He was a learned teacher of the law, with an approach that required strict adherence to many rules. He had observed that Jesus had been doing miracles that could not otherwise be explained, and therefore deduced that God had sent Him as a teacher.

Jesus responded to him by saying that in order to see spiritual things it is necessary to be born from above [ie born spiritually] or to be 'born again'. Nicodemus interpreted Jesus' comments literally, and questioned how someone could go back into their mother's womb. Jesus clarified that He was talking about a different type of birth: a spiritual birth rather than a second physical birth. He went on to explain that God sent His only Son to save us, and give us eternal life. Within these few verses, Jesus communicated three truths: 1) We

1 John 3:1-21

are condemned because of our lack of faith in God 2) God intervened and sent His Son to earth 3) Some people will turn to the light [ie Jesus] and won't be condemned, because of their belief in Jesus.

In this encounter, the entire Good News is summarised. There are no stories. Although Jesus begins with an abstract image - that of being born again - His explanation consists of simple statements. Jesus laid out the facts, and allowed Nicodemus to make up his own mind. This would be considered by many Christians to be the minimum requirements that need to be communicated if someone is to follow Jesus.

The only slightly strange idea is that the imagery of the cross that Jesus alludes to, that of being 'lifted up', though clear in retrospect, would not have been as comprehensible to Nicodemus. But he doesn't ask for further explanation, and Jesus doesn't say what He meant.

There is no Scriptural evidence that Jesus met Nicodemus again, but it appears that Nicodemus did become one of His followers. He spoke out on behalf of Jesus when they sent the temple guards to arrest Him[1]. When Jesus was killed, it was Nicodemus, with Joseph of Arimathea, who prepared Jesus' body for burial[2].

One might consider the dialogue between Jesus and Nicodemus as closer to intellectual debate than a normal conversation between two friends. Although it is not a direct expression of what is called the 'Socratic method', it bears similarities. It also bears similarities to the Jewish method of answering a question with a question: The answer to the question 'What is two plus two?' could be 'What is eight minus four?' As a pharisee, Nicodemus would have been comfortable with this kind of discussion.

This tells us two things. Firstly, Jesus was comfortable with dialogue, including intellectual debate. Secondly, we see that He used an appropriate and culturally relevant method of communicating with the person who came to talk with Him. It is also worthy of note that He started the conversation with a statement that was intended to raise a question in Nicodemus' mind. In media, we would call this a hook.

1 John 7:45-52
2 John 19:38-42

The woman at the well[1]

Jesus dealing with the woman at the well was different, although it started in a similar vein. He engaged her in conversation with an ambiguous reference to living water. She challenged His importance, comparing Jesus to Jacob. Jesus corrected her, claiming to be more important than Jacob. She took the bait and asked for more. Jesus then posed a simple request - go and get your husband. She responded that she didn't have one. Then Jesus, with prophetic insight about her, confirmed that she didn't have one husband, but that she had five in the past and was now living with a man to whom she was not married.

That got her attention, fast. Perhaps to change the subject, she then posed the current knotty theological question between Samaritans and Jews about where to worship. However, Jesus responded by knocking the question sideways. He gave the radical answer that both were wrong, and that communion with God was not about where, but about an imminent new method of direct access to God. She recognised that to be related to the expected Messiah; finally Jesus admitted that He was the Messiah.

The result of this was that she returned to the city, and on the basis of the stranger's unexpected knowledge of her clouded background told everyone to come and meet Jesus. The people poured out of the city to meet Jesus. The net result was that many Samaritans believed in Jesus because of the woman's testimony.

Note that here there are few of the characteristics of the encounter with Nicodemus. Jesus used His omnipotent knowledge to get the attention of the woman. He admitted directly to being the Messiah. People followed Him. There was no talk of condemnation because of sin - despite her evidently sinful lifestyle - and no cryptic reference to the cross. The only reference is to Jesus being the Messiah, and people believed Him.

This communication is meeting the Samaritans in their situation, it was a 'contextualised gem' for them. They were expecting the Messiah, almost with bated breath, although their idea of Messiah was that he would be only a prophet. So communicating to her that He is the expected Messiah would have met her hopes and longings.
PTR

The woman caught in adultery[2]

With the woman caught in the act of adultery, the content of Jesus' communication is very different. When the scribes and pharisees brought the woman to Him, He said nothing.

1 John 4:1-26
2 John 8:1-11

In Islam there is a similar story but the encounter between the woman and the prophet Mohammed happens in secret. Nobody knew. She admitted it only to the prophet Mohammed. He said 'Are you sure?' She said 'Yes'. He didn't ask with whom. She said 'Please punish me for this sin and that punishment will cleanse me'. He said 'Go home and after you have had the baby come back to me.'

After 9 months she went to him. He said 'Go and suckle your baby and then come back to me'.

Two years later she came back to him. 'Please clean me', she appealed. This time he said 'OK' and he punished her till she died.

Someone from the community said she is very bad. The prophet said, 'Her repentance is enough to cleanse all the people in the community'. MAX

Even though they kept badgering Him to tell them what He thought they should do with her, He remained silent. Eventually He said, what has become now a famous one liner, 'If any one of you hasn't sinned, he can be the first person to throw a stone'. The crowd melted away, leaving Jesus alone with the woman.

Then came the critical communication between Jesus and the woman. He asked her if there was anyone still there to condemn her. She responded that there wasn't. He then said, 'Neither do I condemn you.' Then He continued, 'Go now, and leave your life of sin'.

It is obvious that the woman had done something that was worthy of condemnation, but Jesus didn't point that out. He told her to turn away from her sin, but didn't mention anything of the cross, or of following Him, or of His being the Messiah.

In each of these three cases, Jesus interacted with the people concerned. The communication was two-way. It's not really surprising when we think about it. Jesus came to earth to bring God and man back into a relationship. And relationships are concerned very much with communication.

There were only two groups that Jesus appeared not to have much time for - the Scribes and the Pharisees. The Pharisees were a group of religious leaders who looked at the minutiae of what we call the Old Testament and developed systems and structures, based upon their reading, that inhibited people from the kind of relationship God wants with those He calls His people. Although Jesus had His harshest words for these people, and sometimes called them a brood of vipers, He would still engage in dialogue when they came to Him.

Jesus dealing with interruptions

Jesus didn't seem to be concerned about interruptions in the same way we would be. Partly this is cultural. In the Middle East if I am in a meeting with somebody and someone else comes in, then the meeting is stopped to greet the new person. Frequently a new meeting will start, including them, and the agenda of the original meeting is either dropped or postponed. Even in Cyprus this happened with a meeting with my bank manager. When the other person had left, she said it drove her wild, but she could not change the expectations that were deeply embedded into their culture.

One of the best known interruptions of Jesus was when children were brought to him and were obviously causing consternation amongst the disciples[1]. Jesus, on the other hand, tells them not to stop them coming and that we should be like them in our faith.

While Jesus was discussing the theology of fasting and feasting with John's disciples, a ruler arrived with a request that Jesus come and heal his daughter who had just died. Without a pause, Jesus got up and went with the man, and brought his daughter back to life.[2]

Later in Matthew's narrative he tells of a time when Jesus was talking to the crowd and His family arrived, wanting to speak to him. When the message was passed to Him, Jesus used the interruption as a way of communicating the bigger truth that we, His disciples, are now His family. It is those who share the same Father in heaven who are brothers and sisters.[3]

Nowhere do I read Jesus silencing people who interrupted. He took each interjection as a further way of communicating His message. They were opportunities for dialogue. It is almost like He valued interruptions as they gave linkage to real life. This fits with the Jewish approach to God, where He is involved in everything.

It is at variance to Plato's teaching and the understanding that many of that period had, where reality and God were supposed to operate on different planes. We have inherited much of our understanding from the ancient Greeks and thus face the same danger - of separating the physical from the spiritual and of so creating a value structure that is alien to the entire history of God's dealing with mankind. We talk about incarnation - God becoming flesh - almost like an alien concept. Yet the very reason for the Incarnation was God's desire that we realise He has always, is always and will always be intimately interested in us as people: mind, body and spirit.

The prophet Mohammed also had to deal with interruptions - he was often asked 'When will be the end of time? One year, 10 years, 100 years?'

I think there is a difference between Christianity and Islam, for instance if I interrupt an imam, he will answer me... but if I disagree with an imam, ALL the people will be upset. Generally asking questions is no problem in Islam...

Contrast with questions in a sermon, if I entered a church and heard them saying 'Jesus is Son of God' I could not question or interrupt. I would be told to go to the mosque... MAX

Jesus telling stories

In looking at the way Jesus used stories to communicate with his audience, we will look at two parables: The parable of the lost son and the parable of the king's wedding banquet.

1 Mark 10:13-16
2 Matthew 9:18-26
3 Matthew 12:46-50

Jesus said that He used parables as a way of enabling those who understood about the Kingdom of God to understand the real meaning, while others would hear them but not understand.

Jesus' parables can be considered to be metaphors: a method of explaining an abstract concept in terms of a real life experience.

There is a story of the king who made a law and the kings son broke the law. The king will take the punishment on myself. He has to do what he promised.

There are two types of promise in Islam 'wahd', a promise of a gift and 'waeed' a promise of punishment. If I promise to give you something, I have to do it but I don't have to do the 'waeed', the promise of punishment. I am free to show mercy.

If the king forgave, he is not bad or a liar, he is merciful. Giving money to son was 'wahd' - he had to give him. And not punishing is based on 'waeed'.

The story is not so shocking at all to the majority of people from the Middle East, many would expect the father to forgive the son. MAX

The parable of the lost son

The parable of the lost son comes as the final part of a trilogy of stories[1] Jesus told about things and people that were lost: The lost sheep, the lost coin and the lost son.

The third story has become probably the best known of Jesus stories. A father had two sons and the younger asked for and got his share in the inheritance and went off to a distant country where he squandered the money in reckless living. When he reached the bottom of the pit he came to his senses and decided to return to his father, admit his errors and ask his father to accept him back as a hired worker.

Even before the son got back to deliver his prepared speech, the father ran out to greet the son and welcomed him back as a son that was lost but now found. He prepared a big celebration for his son. The older son was furious when he found out what had happened. He was jealous of the lavish love shown by his father to his brother. The father reminded him that he still had his inheritance, but encouraged him to rejoice that his brother was back.

This story has been retold again and again through the ages as an example of the grace of God towards us. Indeed, probably more theology has been developed as a result of this story than any of the direct teaching Jesus did during his time on earth.

Because it comes as part of a trilogy about lost items, it's clear that Jesus was trying to reinforce the idea of God seeking us out. He clarified this at the end of the first story, that of the lost sheep, when He said, 'There will be more joy in heaven over one sinner who repents than over ninety-nine respectable people who don't need to repent.'

I have heard it said that Jesus was retelling a story that was in circulation while He was on earth. The original story, so it is believed, had the father rejecting the son when he returned. The motive for that story would have been to

1 Luke 15:1-32

encourage people towards not sinning in the first place, as there is no way back if you do! If it is true that there was this other story, then his listeners would have thought, 'I know this one... I know how it goes,' and would have found the new ending a shock.

Whether He modified an existing story or created a new one out of nothing, most respectable people would have been expecting some sort of penalty to be incurred by the wayward son for his misdemeanours. So the twist at the end would have been a surprise. Since neither of the two preceding stories in the trilogy have this twist, it is clear that Jesus is developing a theme, taking His audience along a step at a time. The lost sheep and the lost coin both allowed the audience to see the personal value in looking for the lost item. The audience thus saw them from the seeker's point of view.

The third story develops the theme, but then takes it from the point of view of the son who is lost; so we see grace at work. Grace is the new addition and the point He is trying to make.

Note that in this story, and in the other two parables in the trilogy, Jesus didn't quote or refer to Scripture. The stories stood alone. They communicated truth about God that didn't contradict Scripture, but was compatible with and supported by truths that could be seen in Scripture. The listeners were allowed to think and discuss their meaning without explanation.

As Muslims we cannot take our religion from stories that someone else tells us. We take our religion from the Qu'ran and the Hadith.

You won't convince someone by a story. But if I am one of many, many people who watch a play or hear a story I will be affected by it. What we need to do is affect people not convince them. MAX

The parable of the king's wedding banquet

People often associate the text from Matthew 22, the parable of the wedding banquet, with the text from Luke 14, which is very similar. Luke's version doesn't mention a wedding being the motive for the banquet, nor does it have the same ending. It's the version in Matthew[1] that we shall look at.

Jesus tells this story about a king planning a wedding banquet for his son. When the king sent out his servants to the feast, the guests paid scant attention to them or even worse, beat them up and killed them. Understandably, the king was angry and he sent soldiers to ransack and kill the original guests. He then sent out other servants to invite as many people as possible, good and bad alike, so that his banqueting hall would be full.

1 Matthew 22:1-14

When it was full, the king came to greet the guests. He saw one person there who didn't have on wedding clothes. The king's reaction to this seems shocking; The king tells his servants to tie up the man so he cannot escape, and throw him out of the feast into the dark.

This has become probably my favourite parable of those that Jesus told. A few years ago I was sitting in a restaurant beside the Nile in Cairo and discussing this story with a Middle Eastern friend. It was that friend who explained the cultural insight that makes sense of this story that had troubled me for many years. Apparently, it was a Middle Eastern custom for the host of a wedding banquet to provide special clothes for the guests to wear. This was partly a gift for the guests, and also a leveller, so that guests would all be equal. In the story, the fact that the king finds a guest in the hall not wearing wedding clothes implies that the guest wanted what he could get from the king in terms of filling his belly, without wanting to really be part of the celebration.

The fact that the story vexed me and made me think for years is one of the reasons storytelling is so effective. It engages us in the activity of understanding. If the story had been plain and simple I would probably not have come back to it again and again, pondering it in my mind. As it was, the puzzling made me think, and the discovery of the meaning has burned the truth that Jesus wanted to communicate deeper into my being than it would otherwise.

The interesting comparison between the two stories is that there is in each almost a false ending. In the story of the lost son, the story could end when the lost son is accepted back by his father. In the story of the king's banquet, the story could end with the new guests coming into the banquet and the king accepting them.

We have a technique in media called 'story lining' where we draw diagrams to show the build-up of tension within a story, or coloured lines to show the parts and interactions which different characters play. Generally a story ends just after the climax, often with a few loose ends to be tied up. However, in these two stories, tying up the loose ends changes the entire meaning of each story.

In the story of the lost son, the second ending tells us that even though the wayward son was accepted back, those who have been with God all the time must not be jealous and that they will still inherit eternal life. In the story of the king's banquet, the second ending tells us that even though

As a Muslim, after watching a movie like the Jesus film, I will feel that I have sinned in some way. But many, many people don't notice that and so you can affect people - to show and to let them feel rather than think. Drama stories will push them second or third time to hear the message of God even though it doesn't convince them. MAX

we have been accepted into the banquet it is on the basis of the covering that God provides rather than on the basis of his invitation.

The stories are almost ageless, and people have told and retold them down through the centuries. Recently we helped dub 'Lost and Found', a film version of the trilogy of the stories about the lost, into the Farsi language. This is a ninety minute drama, taking the three Biblical stories as their basis and expanding upon them. I often wonder to what extent we have précis of the stories that Jesus told, or if they are verbatim.

Jesus teaching people

There are relatively few examples of Jesus giving direct teaching. We see asides or comments at the end of stories as direct communication, like at the end of the story of the lost sheep, but mostly He communicated through stories or dialogue. We will consider two examples: Firstly the most famous teaching Jesus did, that we now call the 'Sermon on th Mount'[1] and secondly Jesus teaching at the synagogue in Capernaum[2].

The Sermon on th Mount

The Sermon on th Mount is the longest record of any of Jesus' teaching, spanning three chapters in Matthew's narrative. The account of this talk ranges over many topics, and covers a number of different styles of teaching: the almost poetic series of quotes starting 'Blessed are…', metaphor and similes, interpretation and explanation of the law, teaching about prayer and about the Kingdom in general.

I suspect that the Sermon on th Mount may have been a series of smaller talks that Jesus gave over a period of time during that day, not a straightforward verbatim account of a single talk. The reason I say this is that there are so many disparate topics in this teaching that it would have been difficult for his audience to remember them.

Regardless of whether it was a single talk or a series of shorter talks given in one session with the crowd on the mountain, we can see that it bears little resemblance to a modern evangelical sermon. There are not three points, there

1 Matthew 5:1-7:29
2 John 6:25-59

are no amusing anecdotes, there is relatively little quoting of Scripture, there is not one single subject.

The structure of Jesus' talk falls into five sections: The poetic opening, an interpretation of the law, patterns for prayer, encouragement to be sold out for God and to bear fruit. He ended with a short story, the parable of the house built on sand. When He interpreted the law, He did it in a totally different way to the religious leaders of the time.

Jesus focused on what we would call the spirit of the law rather than the letter of the law. In fact that could almost be seen as his unifying theme to the Sermon on th Mount: It's the principles that matter rather than the detail.

We see here also a difference between teaching and preaching. Jesus was teaching about the life of following God. He was not telling parables, nor was He in dialogue, prior to following Him. However, He uses metaphors and similes when appropriate. Though He encourages people in their life for God, His starting point is an assumption that they are His followers.

Teaching at the synagogue in Capernaum

Jesus' talk in the synagogue in Capernaum was very different in style to the Sermon on th Mount. In this talk He used different repeated metaphors related to food.

He started off by chastising His listeners for following Him looking for miraculous provision of food, encouraging them to look instead for spiritual food. He claimed to be the bread of life, fulfilling everyone's spiritual hunger and thirst. Finally, He predicted what we call the communion or Eucharist, by referring to eating His body and drinking His blood.

The Bible tells us that this was while teaching in the synagogue, yet we can see things very different from a modern sermon. This talk appeared to be more dialectic than didactic.

Didactic teaching implies a form of teacher driven communication whereas dialectic implies a form of learning using dialogue. There are two differences - didactic focusing of the delivery of the message contrasted with dialectic focusing on the understanding of the message and secondly contrasting didactic monologue with dialectic dialogue. Jesus appeared to focus on the understanding of the message and allowed for or encouraged dialogue.

In Jesus teaching at the synagogue in Capernaum there

were interruptions, there was dialogue, there were grumblings and arguments. It doesn't sound like our polite way of sitting and listening to a talk on a Sunday morning. But Jesus didn't appear to be put off by the interjections. Instead he welcomed them as part of the way to convey what He wanted to teach.

Models of the church, becoming a follower of Jesus and how it happens...

We sometimes try to make sense of the world around us through abstract thought. This allows us to create internal representations of what we see, hear, and feel. We call these representations 'models'. They can help us to simplify complex concepts.

Even if you don't like 'models', try to bear with them, thinking of them in terms of descriptions of the way some people engage in evangelistic activity. They are helpful in understanding other perspectives in our common aim of bringing people into the gathering of Jesus' followers.

There are various models describing how people become followers of Jesus, which match differing theologies. There are three broad models: The *Outside/Inside* model, the *Process* model and the *Orientation* model. We developed a fourth *Composite* model combining both the Process model and the Orientation model.

What should be borne in mind with all models is that they are only that: models. They are representations of reality, which aim to help us make sense of it, and also to help us in our approach to evangelism and building the Body of Christ.

Every model is flawed in some way, yet they all help to give a picture of what is essentially a mystery: how God reconciled man to Himself.

Outside/Inside Model

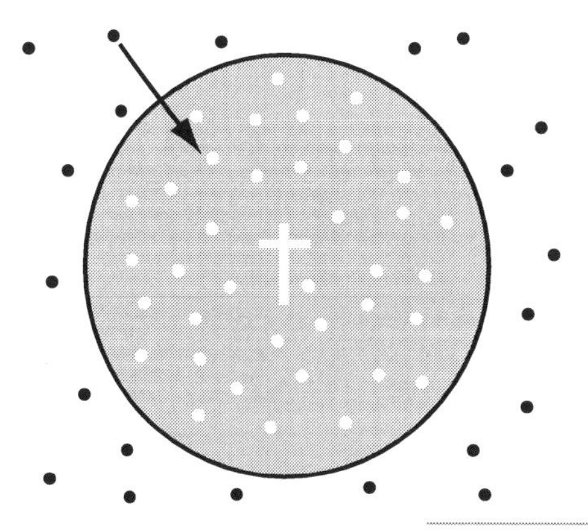

The Outside/Inside Model is the simplest of the three. It basically states you are either a member of the Body of Christ, or you are outside it.

Almost all Christian traditions and backgrounds hold that some people are Christians [or followers of Jesus] and some are not. Some teach that nobody goes looking for God; that it is exclusively God calling man that starts the process, and that men are chosen despite themselves. Others believe that man does seek God, and that He knows beforehand who those will be. Some believe that as soon as we are saved there is no going back: whatever we do after that we will go to heaven and be with God for eternity. Others hold that it is an ongoing

My experience was there was too little follow up and discipleship! Before I was a believer, the Christian I was in contact with went away for two months. This was very sad for me as I needed him a lot at this time. I was not yet a believer and he sent someone else as a deputy to meet me in his place...

At the first meeting this person said 'This is too early in the day to meet, can we meet later...' That had been a good time for me but reluctantly I agreed.

At the second meeting he challenged me 'Do you accept Jesus now?' and I replied 'No, not yet' And from then on he failed to turn up to the meetings.

When the original Christian came back, I met him in the street and said 'Why did the meetings stop?' He replied, 'I was told you didn't want to meet any more...', 'No, I have no idea where he got that idea.' I expressed surprise and said, 'I came many times and didn't find him'. He said, 'OK, we can meet if you want'.

I felt he should have come to me and found out what had happened. Bringing someone from the Middle East to a relationship with Jesus is a process and takes time. MAX

belief in God that saves us rather than a one-time act.

Still, despite these variations in belief, most are agreed that some are 'inside' the Body, and some are 'outside'. There is much Scriptural evidence for this basic model. Jesus talked of those who were 'for Him' and those 'against Him' as two mutually exclusive groups[1]. Paul wrote of those who were 'in the world' contrasted with 'brothers'[2]. The book of Revelation contrasts those whose names are written in the Book of Life[3] with those who are thrown into the pit of fire[4].

Often people will cite the story Jesus told of the sheep and the goats, and the separation of people at the end of time either to His left or to His right[5]. The problem with this story is that the parable appears to link inside and outside to social concerns rather than faith. Some people, therefore, interpret the story as relating exclusively to those who already have faith and are followers of Jesus. Others interpret it as referring to those who have never heard of Jesus at all.

When people follow the Inside/Outside model narrowly, their one aim is to 'get people from outside to inside'; the way they do so is less important than the result.

At its most basic, people are considered to move from outside the Body to inside either by saying some special prayer [the so-called 'sinners prayer'], by doing a prescribed set of actions [such as the 'ABC's of salvation'] or an external event [such as Baptism]. The problem with this is that many people reject the message, and some who apparently take this first step show no signs of following Jesus afterwards. This can be very discouraging for those trying to reach out to unbelievers.

In evaluating media for evangelism or discipleship, however, this model is not really helpful at all. We know from experience that people outside and inside see things in very different ways. Thus, media created by 'insiders' using insider language could - at best - not communicate, or - worse - miscommunicate the truth and good news about Jesus to 'outsiders'.

In the Middle East the term 'Christian' is particularly unhelpful, since it could either mean someone born into that cultural background, or possibly even everyone in the West.

1 Matthew 19:29-31
2 1 Corinthians 5
3 Revelation 20:11-13
4 Revelation 20:14-15
5 Matthew 25

Process Model

The process model is derived from the outside/inside model, but describes belief in Jesus and discipleship as a process rather than a single life-changing event. Jesus called people to follow Him; but most, if not all, of the early disciples realised the truth about Him only after they had become His followers. There were stages in the disciples' understanding about Jesus – even Peter, one of His closest friends, did not fully understand who Jesus was until He had been with him for a considerable time[1]. Even then He didn't understand the need for Jesus to die. Their decision to follow Him came before their understanding about Him.

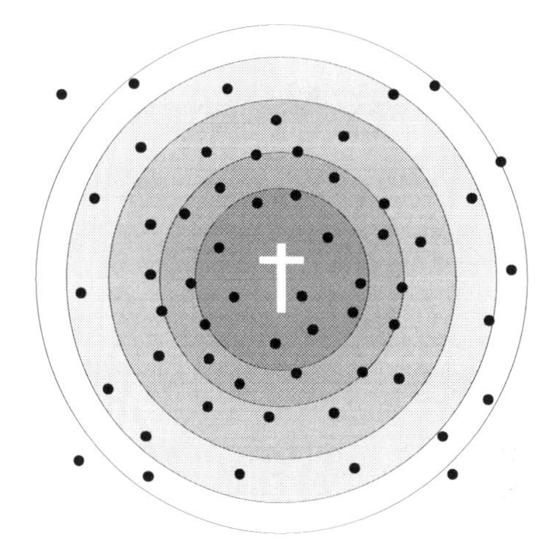

I gather that the Jewish education system was basic primary education, with boys learning by heart the Torah, the law. If kids were very good at that, they would go on to learn more of what we now call the Old Testament, and the rest would become apprenticed to either their father's work or another manual work of some kind. If they were the best of the best they would request an interview with a Rabbi; if he believed they could make it to become a Rabbi themselves and would spread his interpretation of Scripture, he would say to them to 'Lech Acharai – Come, follow him'. They would then leave everything and follow their Rabbi, learning from him and taking on his way of interpreting the Old Testament.

It is into that context that Jesus called His disciples. It was something they had seen and heard about in their daily lives. The best of the best were called to follow a Rabbi. What was unique about Jesus' call was that He believed in many who were not the best of the best. Two of them were young fishermen, apprenticed to their dad, yet Jesus called them to follow Him and they did[2]. They did not pray a prayer of repentance or follow any structured steps. They simply left their nets and went with Jesus.

James Engel wrote a book entitled, 'What's Gone Wrong with the Harvest?' which challenged the Outside/Inside model. He proposed what he called the 'Engel Scale of Spiritual Decision' and he approached it as being a journey, where a person takes a step at a time.

1 Luke 9
2 Matthew 4:21-22

Thinking about this scale, if I am at step -8 but moving toward step -7 am I a follower of Jesus or am I only a follower after 0, when I become a new creature? This question is especially relevant if we think about the disciples deciding to follow Jesus before they realised He is the Messiah.
PTR

Below is a table showing the steps:

-8	Awareness of Supreme Being but no effective knowledge of the Gospel
-7	Initial awareness of the Gospel
-6	Awareness of Fundamentals of the Gospel
-5	Grasp of Implications of Gospel
-4	Positive attitude Toward Gospel
-3	Personal Problem Recognition
-2	DECISION TO ACT
-1	Repentance and Faith in Christ
	NEW CREATURE
+1	Post-Decision Evaluation
+2	Incorporation into Body
+3	Conceptual and Behavioural Growth
+4	Communion with God
+5	Stewardship
	Reproduction
	Internally (gifts, etc)
	Externally (witness, social action, etc)

This model does not focus on a 'do it now' approach of pressuring people into a decision. It allows them to be anywhere on the scale, taking steps towards following Jesus. The process model is most easily shown as a series of concentric circles, putting each person into one of them depending on where they are in the process.

With this model, the aim in witnessing or evangelism is to move someone from an outer circle to one of those closer to the centre. Implicit within the model is that people are moving from further out to further in. Because of the way the scale is described, it doesn't model well people who might be heading in the opposite direction.

The Engel scale has been taken and adapted by various people, but still reflects the basic Process model of following Jesus.

It can be helpful when evaluating media for use in evangelism, since it helps us to say, 'this would be good for someone at this place in their journey'. However, the scale is heavily western-oriented in its approach to God. To evaluate media used for outreach and discipling of people in the Middle East, we had to develop a Middle Eastern version of it.

Orientation Model

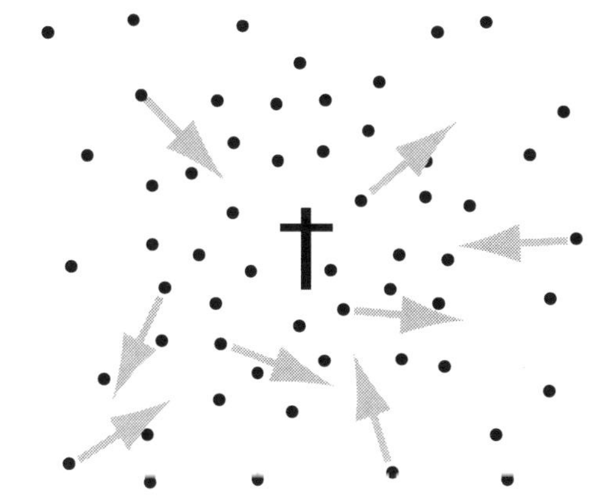

The Orientation Model focuses not on the position of the person, but the direction they are travelling. This is best expressed by the following diagram, where the circles have been removed, and the direction of travel is indicated.

There are recorded instances when Jesus called people to follow Him, yet they decided not to. For instance, one person said they wanted to first bury their father; in other words, wait till later when their father had died, before following[1]. Another said they wanted to ask if it was all right with their family[2]. To me this shows that the direction we face or the direction we are travelling spiritually is at least as important as where we are spiritually. Each was at a crossroads, and each was choosing a direction.

The Bible shows that there can be confusion about who is and who is not a follower, and what their relationship is to Jesus. Consider the person that the disciples saw casting out demons in Jesus' name: They told the person to stop because he was not part of their group, ie not an insider. Yet Jesus said to allow them to continue, since everyone who is not against Him was for Him[3]. This causes ambiguity, since many of us would love it to be clear who is part of the church or who is not. Yet Jesus appears to allow for ambiguity.

What is important in this model is not whether a person is 'in' or 'out' but whether they are heading towards or away from Jesus. It allows for some people to be a long way away from Jesus but heading towards Him, and others to be relatively close to Him, but heading away. Hence this model implies that it's a good idea to nurture and encourage everyone towards Jesus, whereever they are, rather than judging whether they are 'inside' or 'outside'.

This matches some of our experiences with people outside the church appearing to show significant interest in the Lord, while others inside the church do not exhibit very Christ-like characteristics. It encourages us not to judge whether someone is inside or outside, but to inspire all people wherever they are towards a loving God who desires a relationship with them.

1 Luke 9:60
2 Luke 9:61-62
3 Luke 9:50

This model works particularly well for the people we might describe as 'natural evangelists,' since whenever they meet people they tend to encourage them to head towards Jesus. It's also helpful for the rest of us, as it allows us to witness or share in a more natural way, without putting any pressure on us to see someone 'be converted' (with the Inside/Outside model) or 'move up a level' (with the Process model).

However, the Orientation Model is not very helpful in evaluating media for use in evangelism and discipleship, since what is appropriate to someone is more likely to be related to their position than to the direction they are heading.

These, then, are the three generally understood models that are mostly used by people involved in evangelism or church-planting. They all have some Scriptural basis, and they all have limitations.

There are, however, two further models, one of which we developed ourselves, and the other sometimes expressed in a different way by people who are unhappy with models at all.

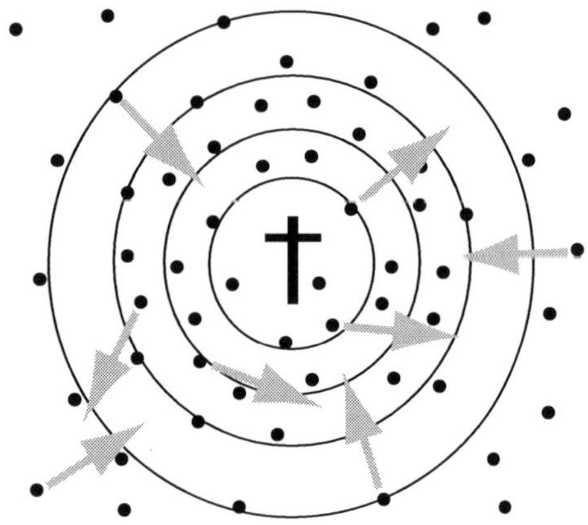

Looking at this model, is it more obvious if someone has changed direction or if they have moved forward in the same direction?
PTR

Composite Process/Orientation Model

The composite model superimposes the Process model with the Orientation model. In other words, we observe where someone is in relationship to Jesus, but wherever they are we are more concerned about the direction they are heading than their position.

Jesus talked about the Kingdom coming close to someone[1]. In that case, if the Kingdom comes close to them, they must be close to the Kingdom. Similarly there must be some people further away. Although it is not specified, there is some measure of proximity.

Alongside this, in the Bible we read of people who appear to be close yet are almost certainly not in the Kingdom. The most obvious example of this would be Judas Iscariot. He was so much a part of the inside group that, during the Last Supper, the other disciples didn't know that he was going to betray Jesus[2]. Ananias and Sapphira are another example[3]. This model allows media to be evaluated according to the Process model, while focusing on pointing people toward Jesus rather than worrying about whether they are moving up the ladder in the process.

1 Luke 10:8-12
2 Luke 22:1-38
3 Acts 5:1-11

John Finney in his book *Emerging Evangelism* admits this:

> *My own research into what actually happened to people who became Christians showed that it was a more complicated process than had been supposed and also that it often took place over a period of time, sometimes many years... On the Way was published in 1995. The title is indicative of the new thinking. Becoming a follower of Jesus was no longer seen as a sudden decision by an individual who stepped from unfaith to faith in a moment but as a pilgrimage where each individual came to faith by a different journey.'*[1]

This 'pilgrimage' I believe is best expressed in the composite process/orientation model.

Relationship Model

The final model to consider is the relationship model. The best way to see this is as a bungee cord attached between God and every individual person on the planet. That cord represents the relationship between them. It's something that can be stretched till it appears to be almost breaking. The bungee cord can be in any direction and any length. This model allows for a very ambiguous relationship between God and man.

Jesus seemed to deal with each person in a unique way. To fishermen He said, 'Follow me and I will teach you how to catch people instead of fish'[2]. To a teacher and thinker He said, 'You must be born from above'[3]. To a woman caught in the act of adultery He said, 'Don't do it again'[4]. To a woman He met at a well, 'Come and drink of the water of life'[5]. This variety of dealings with people seemed to take account of where they were in their relationship with Jesus, yet they were never too far away to be outside His care.

We understand these passages in retrospect, seeing the whole of the New Testament. Yet each individual at the time got only a small part of the message. Because we see in

I like the idea of bungee cord. Way more than the Engel "Steps" idea. I see some people who go from "Gospel? God? Huh?" to a Born-again completely changed-life in about 10 minutes. I guess that's like God pulling on his end of the cord, and the bungee taking effect and them zipping up to Him. Then others who stay miles away for ages, I guess that's like Him having to spin them around and around to get up speed before he can bring them in. Pulling too fast might snap the cord.
DAN

1 Emerging Evangelism - John Finney - page 76-77
2 Matthew 4:19
3 John 3:1-21
4 John 8:1-11
5 John 4:1-26

retrospect, we frequently try to incorporate everything into our communication about the Lord – yet that didn't happen in Scripture.

The same could be said of Paul, where he deliberately chooses a unique approach in each context. Contrast, for instance, his talks to Jewish and Greek people. We can read of his talk in the synagogue in Pisisian Antioch in Acts 13 and his talk to Greeks in Athens in Acts 17. This was not an accidental difference, Paul says that he became Jewish for Jewish people and like a gentile for those who are not Jewish in order to win them for Christ[1].

Jesus talked about the Kingdom of God, or the Kingdom of Heaven[2]. In Arabic there are two words for Kingdom: malakoot [used in the context of the kingdom of God] and memlekah [used in the context of the kingdom of Saudi Arabia]. In English we have only the word kingdom, and can get confused about its meaning. Frequently we see it more in territorial terms than spiritual ones, and we therefore have a fuzzy understanding the Kingdom of God.

There are times when I look at people I know, and at the Bible, and think that the relationship model is the only one that really expresses what I see. However, in terms of evaluating media for use in evangelism it is not particularly helpful. So, overall, despite its flaws, I tend to find the composite orientation/process model the most useful.

Models and the church

Every follower of Jesus is a member of the body of Christ, whether a secret believer in a country where they decide not to openly admit to being a Christian, or an attender at a church in a country which is free and democratic. We tend to more commonly call the Body of Christ the church. So these models can also been seen as models of entry into the church.

Some of the models, for instance the outside/inside model, appear to fit better with our understanding of church. Some, for instance the orientation model, appear difficult to reconcile with an understanding of the church as some sort of organisation. The church has been seen in terms or organisation, and often in terms of the building that is used for the Sunday meeting, for the vast majority of the time

1 1 Corinthians 9:19-23
2 Matthew 4:17

since Jesus was on earth. To what extent that is what He intended is open to discussion.

When we look at the models, thinking about them in terms of how well they model the church, I think using the phrase 'the Body of Christ' will help our understanding. Alongside this we need to think how they might affect potential new gatherings of Jesus-followers who come from a background very different to that of the West.

It was Jesus' custom to go to the synagogue on the Sabbath and He didn't reject the Jewish customs, even though he sometimes overruled the petty laws developed by the Pharisees. However, when speaking with the woman at the well in Samaria, He clearly prophesied that the time was coming when external characteristics of worship would be irrelevant. I therefore think that some of the models that don't match comfortably with our perceptions of church, and yet have Biblical basis, should be seen as a challenge to our perception of church rather than rejected.

Communication Theory

The 'Engel Scale of Spiritual Decision' (see page 19) describes the way in which an individual or group progress in their understanding of the Gospel as God reveals Himself to them. Thus by understanding the way God communicates, we can become better co-communicators. Hence, although it was not shown in the simplified table above, the scale has columns to show what God's role is at each stage and what the communicator's role is alongside this. The communicator is the evangelist sharing the Gospel. These columns can be very helpful in our evangelism and praying for people.

Because the communication is seen as important in the process, looking at communication theory is also important, if we are to do it to our best ability. When looking at media, be it a printed tract, a TV programme or website, communication theory is critical to what we do. However, there are some perceived errors in looking at the Engel Scale. Take, for instance, the communicator's role between -8 and -2, which is listed as 'Proclamation'.

It's possibly confusing to people involved in media to have the communicators' role defined as 'proclamation' and 'persuasion' between -7 and -1 and then 'follow-up' from +1 to +3 since we usually refer to the activity of responding to inquirers between -7 and -1 as 'follow-up'.
PTR

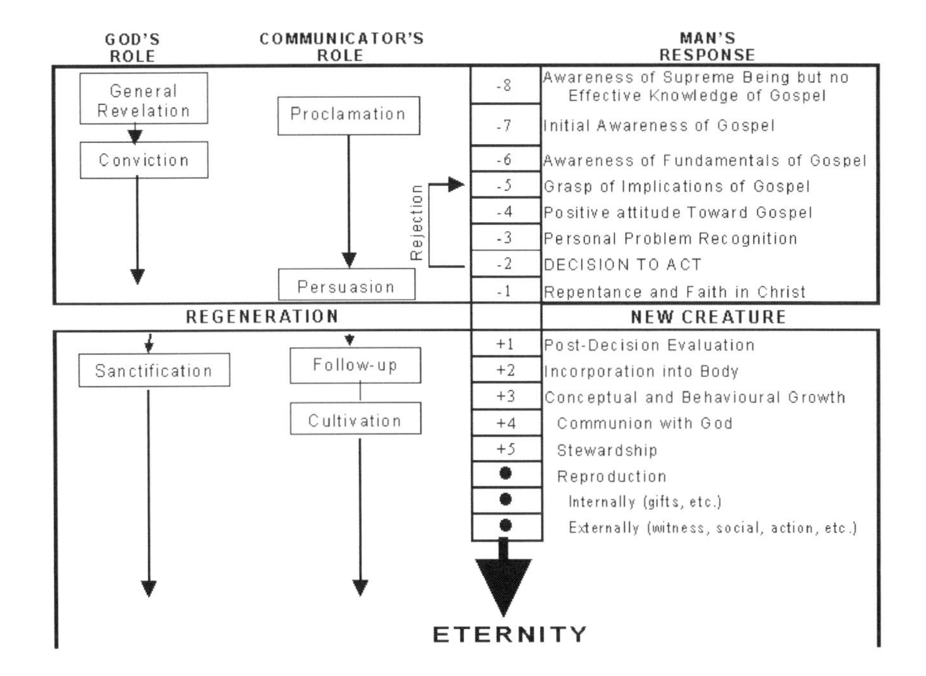

These noises can hide or reduce the message, however, there can also be positive noises in these areas which resonate with and amplify the message. We are not always dependent on one source for the message and this can effectively also amplify the message
PTR

And of course, God often sprinkles in 'noise' of His own when we don't transmit the message the receiver needs to hear. Unfortunately, a lot of gospel proclamation I've seen tends towards relying completely on God's noise. Yes, God does do the saving work, not us, but we have no excuse for broadcasting nonsense in the expectation that God will turn it around all the time. Why then would God want us to transmit at all?
DAN

Proclamation is seen by many as a one way process: We proclaim, they listen. Traditionally, radio evangelism has worked that way. What radio evangelists call 'follow up' is really what is listed under the communicator's role in -1, that of persuasion.

The Shannon-Weaver and Lasswell models of communication are called 'transmission' models of communication. These two models come out of American research and show what is called a Source-Message/Channel-Receiver process of communication. It, like the proclamation above, is orientated toward a unidirectional flow of information. However, it's useful to look at it since it does have some valuable insights into potential problems. The following diagram comes from Claude E Shannon and Warren Weaver, The Mathematical Theory of Communication[1]

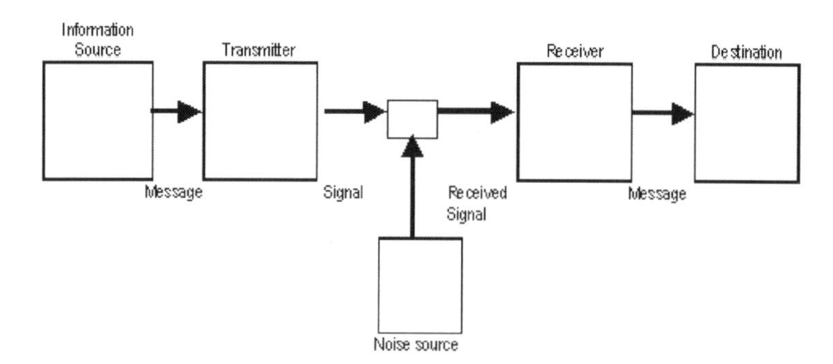

This model, which was originally devised to help a US telephone company while thinking about fidelity of reproduction, has now become a widely accepted tool in human inter-personal communication. What is important to realise in communication is that the receiver does not necessarily get what we send. Even standing beside someone, the 'noise source', which can be their cultural conditioning, may render communication wildly inaccurate.

The 'noise' that can hinder communication can be one of three forms: cultural, spiritual or personal. This can be compared to what Christians often refer to as 'the world, the flesh and the devil'. In both cases, although these are separate, they often overlap in a confusing manner since we are complex human beings.

When I refer to cultural noise I mean the context in which we live. In a secularised Western context, this could be a

1 Urbana, Illinois, University of Illinois Press, 1949 - p. 9

perception that God either doesn't exist, or is irrelevant, or a fable. Post-modern young people could see God as existing *for you*, but not for them. You could argue that He is God for everyone, and they would respond that *for you* He is God for everyone! The cultural noise is blocking the communication.

When I refer to personal noise, I am thinking of personal experiences which may influence the hearer. This could be a bad experience with Christians in the past. Or it could be a personal misperception. For instance, if you refer to God as 'our Father' and a person had an abusive father, that person will likely think you are trying to communicate that God is abusive.

Spiritual noise can be directly from Satan or a demon blocking the communication or adding in noise. Whether the filter in the middle is adding noise or subtracting from the signal the effect is the same: the quantity and quality of the signal compared to the noise is impaired.

One person I was talking to about this said that the cultural and personal noise could also be considered as types of spiritual noise. Whether we see them as separate or all as types of spiritual noise is irrelevant to the point I am trying to make: there are forms of noise which hinder the communication of the Gospel.

With all those noise sources, the question facing people trying to communicate the Gospel is, 'How do I know they have heard and understood?' The answer of course is feedback. At least, that's the technical word for it. I might prefer to call it dialogue. I speak, you listen. You speak, I listen. This doesn't guarantee accuracy of communication, but it radically improves it, especially if we learn how to really listen.

There is also the 'noise' from well-meaning but misguided Christians, or from inappropriate church services or meetings.

The secular world has taken this on board, but Christian communicators are lagging behind. Rarely does an hour go by without a secular radio station having some form of communication for the listener into the programme, either from a phone call, SMS message or email, but this is seldom the case with Christian radio. There are exceptions to this: one Christian radio station I know makes its daily programme almost exclusively from interaction with the audience through SMS messages.

Noise can be words from the people against Christianity – there are a lot of false accusations. People say, 'Christianity is not good', so it becomes impossible to see it as good. Laziness is another problem – they don't want to think – for instance if my imam says this or that I am then convinced what he says is correct and I don't want to think about the truth. I don't want to think about this, I'm a Muslim and I don't want to think. MAX

In *Tell it Often, Tell it Well*, Mark McCloskey & Bill Bright express it this way:

1. *An emphasis on feedback ensures a dialogue, a two-way process of honest interaction, instead of a monologue, a one-way flow of information. The listener becomes part of the communication process and, as a result, his mind, heart and will are more likely to be engaged in reasoning through the personal implications of the gospel.*

2. *Feedback can help you improve the accuracy of your message transmission. We must always ask ourselves, "Has the listener truly understood what I have said, or have noise and the hazards of decoding robbed my message of its fidelity?" Feedback lets you know if the listener has heard what you meant him to hear. You will be able to evaluate how much he has truly understood the gospel. As we have already learned, this matter is crucial if we are to persuade and not propagandise, if we are to call clearly for Spirit-led, life-changing decisions for Christ and not settle for shallow, spurious responses masquerading as saving faith.*

3. *Feedback can help you keep the conversation personally relevant to the listener. It helps you determine his receptivity to the gospel message. Is the information causing the listener to ask the right kind of questions, the kind that are answered only in the cross of Christ? Is he ready for more information? Is he ready to decide for Christ? The communicator who is committed to effectiveness will place a high priority on encouraging and interpreting feedback.*

4. *To rob the listener of the opportunity for feedback is tantamount to saying, "I don't care what you think about this, just let me talk". This attitude not only hinders the evangelist from accurately handling the word of truth, but also insults the listener's person hood. We must respond to the listener as an individual and relate the value of the gospel to his life situation, speaking to any barriers to his full understanding of the personal implications of the gospel. Feedback is essential in this process.*

What surprises me is that this book was published in 1985, and yet more than 20 years later it has had very little impact upon Christian communication. However, it does parallel the change in the UK away from mass evangelistic events to a more dialogue-based small group evangelism that has taken place over those 20 years.

One reason why in media this has been ignored is a fear I have heard expressed, that if we allow listeners to speak they might say things we don't want them to. Another person told me we should make programmes that ***look like they are live*** and have interaction, ***but are actually recorded...*** so we can control them. Though this might mimic the interactive programmes of the secular media, it would remove the feedback path and so diminish the quality of the communication.

There is an interesting book by John Finney called 'Emerging Evangelism', which is worth reading. In the book, Finney charts the history of evangelism.

Proclamation/mass evangelism as we know it dates from Charles Finney (1792-1875). The fires of the First Awakening under Jonathan Edwards had 'burnt themselves out' and in the 1790s 'revivalist' meetings took place first on the west coast of America and then moved East. Charles Finney put structure into these meetings and they became broadly what we know to be the mass evangelism meetings of today.'

John Finney lists Reinhard Bonnke, Billy Graham and Luis Palau [and many others] as following Charles Finney's techniques and principles. The method is simple - the message is proclaimed [one way], the audience hears the word of God, people make a decision [repent] and believe. Task complete.

This method continued in the UK, until approximately 1985. However by the year 2000 what was taking place in the UK had radically changed. This method that had prevailed for about 200 years had been completely turned around. It was not a conscious change and John Finney says 'it happened without anyone really noticing it'. Partly this was because the culture of the UK had changed, but the real reason was, Finney puts it, 'basically, it did not work'.

The assertion that it 'did not work' was not a denial of any people coming to Christ, but was really a comment about the ineffectiveness of mass evangelism. After the Billy Graham campaigns of 1984, 1985 and 1989 in the UK, people sat down to work out how effective they had been. They had certainly given the local churches a 'shot in the arm'; quite a number

When I think of a big group meeting for evangelism, I think it can work if you prepare something special for the Muslims. It's not useful to preach. Maybe give drama, music, something that will touch their hearts. Not long heavy preaching. The problem is the assumption that people are ready to hear and this not really true - drama or humour can communicate a message much stronger than preaching. MAX

If you do end up gathering many hundreds of people... it's very difficult not to take the opportunity and to refuse to talk to the crowd. But how should you try to communicate? You can use drama and music and that will affect them. At the end they are likely to ask if you will do this again and again.

It's a problem to try to 'preach the Gospel' and use the logic needed to convince Muslims. Generally it will not be helpful.
MAX

of people on the edge of the church had found a deeper commitment to God. But although there were some outsiders who had found Christ and become disciples, the numbers were not great.

According to the Billy Graham Evangelistic Association, between 3.5% and 4.5% go forward at a rally[1]. Of those who go forward, they estimate 2% have made a decision to follow Christ during the talk[2]. Billy Graham himself admitted that about 25% of those who make decisions result in long term commitment to the Lord[3]. Taken together these figures show approximately 0.02% of people who come to a rally make a long term commitment during the talk. Billy Graham spoke to about 50 million people in his ministry and that means around 10,000 were converted during his talks.

In the two decades before this, a number of small-group courses were introduced in the UK. These were derived from the confirmation or initiation courses used for teenagers, but the authors of these courses found that they had to be less didactic and more dialogue-based to work with adults. The church we attended in Biringham used courses like '*Good News down your Street*' very effectively. '*Saints Alive!*' came from a church just up the road in Nottingham. These courses had two aims: not only to bring people to faith, but also to let them experience the power of the Holy Spirit.

They were very informal - one example of their use in our church would be in baptism preparation. Being an Anglican church, many people would come there to get their children baptised. The leaders would say that a condition of that was that they should attend a '*Good News down your Street*'. The course took place in their home, so baby-sitters were not necessary, and they felt comfortable.

The course would be run by a couple who were house group leaders plus one other member of that house group, ie five people together. The result of these courses was that the young couple either decided to follow Jesus and would join the house group of the people who they already knew, or they would decide that they didn't want their child baptised anyway.

1 The Closest Thing To A White House Chaplain, Edward B. Fiske, New York Times Magazine, 8 January 1969
2 1994 Christian Life and Witness Course video, Kel Richards, National Coordinator for BGEA Australia
3 Billy Graham - Personal Thoughts of a Public Man, David Frost, pp.71-72

During the Billy Graham campaigns of the 1980s, 'nurture groups' were introduced. These were intended to be groups for people after they became Christians. So those who had gone forward at a rally, could attend and thus be encouraged into a local congregation. Although that was their intention, what people found was that a home-based group was a safe place to share their faith, and that non-Christians would listen and frequently come to faith, in dialogue, rather than as a result of the proclamation.

In 1991 the Decade of Evangelism was started in the UK, and those responsible for steering it decided that the emphasis should be in the 'nurture group' rather than the one-way proclamation evangelism which had been dominant for the preceding 200 years. The Christian press responded with, 'The Decade begins by not evangelising!'. In reality it was the start of the new dialogue-based approach to evangelism.

In 1993 the Alpha course was published by Holy Trinity church in Brompton, and has now become one of the most popular courses used for evangelism in the UK. The method of Alpha is significant. You either meet in a home or church venue. You start by having a meal together - this is considered a critical part of the course. After the meal, there is either a short talk or a video. From that there is one or more discussion groups. The discussion groups have a majority of non-Christians, and the Christian members are taught to listen rather than speak. It flies right in the face of proclamation evangelism, since non-Christians are allowed to voice all their objections and feelings.

But it is true dialogue. And it works. Over 2 million people attended these courses between 1994 and 2004 [that is more than 3% of the population of the UK] and one in six [17%] say that they have become Christians as a result[1]. In other words, more than one third of a million people have become Christians through dialogue-based evangelism in the UK during one decade. This is statistically well over 800 times as effective as large rally-based evangelism.

I don't think Jesus ever had any problems with dialogue and interaction. He had some pretty off-the-wall people come up to him with some wild ideas, but each time He turned them round to be effective ways of communicating His Good News. If we are His followers, we should follow His techniques.

You know, the funny thing is, many Christians want the alpha course to be one directional. They deliberately use the tapes, not a live speaker, so that it becomes as dialectic as possible, with some discussion time afterwards. DAN

1 Emerging Evangelism, John Finney, p79

Scales for measuring media

One of the values we hold is to use some sort of objective criteria to measure the effectiveness of what we do alongside being led by the Holy Spirit. This chapter introduces three scales we have just started using ourselves: Firstly an 'Anti-Christianity to Jesus-follower scale', which is similar in function to the Engel scale but specifically oriented towards working among people in the Middle East. Secondly a cultural contextualisation scale and thirdly a boldness scale.

We want to use these scales for analysing and describing rather than rating media, not as a pejorative 'You're doing this wrong' but for people to say 'My target audience is this...' and then compare with their target to know how well we are doing. For instance, a '*Christian station for the Christians of the Middle East*', quite naturally is likely to be C1, E1-E4 and B7. You will have to read the rest of the chapter to see what we mean by C1, E1-E4 and B7!

The second use of the scales is to enable people to know what might be appropriate to use in sharing the Good News of Jesus for someone at a particular point in their journey of faith.

These scales are not something developed out of extensive research. They were developed as a result of a couple of years of trying various approaches, including some research-based methods and building on the work of others before us. Although they therefore have no research backbone, when we first saw them we realised that they felt right to our experience of developing media tools.

I have felt that our activities and our research are rather like shooting at a moving target from a high speed train. Not only is the culture of the people we are trying to reach changing, but the methods and culture of those doing the reaching is also changing. Thus within these scales there could be errors, so we see them as a work in progress rather than the final solution. Since culture and media are changing so fast, we treat them as a best approximation rather than fact. In the same way that models are representations of reality, these also are representations of reality that help us to make sense of what we are doing.

The scales are useful, but you cannot bring everything correct, but you can catch something and this helps. But to be honest each person is different and is private individual and has different understanding. It's a starting point even with its limitations.

The perfect way to create the scales would be to have many interviews with people and then to study them and create the scales from that. But it encompasses my feelings, my reactions. Some people may disagree with the scales, and others will agree. But we need to catch something and start somewhere and develop it. MAX

This sounds too weak to me! This may not be 'ivory tower' research, which only makes me yawn but is 'over the shoulder' observations we have made of more than twelve media agencies' output, looking at their methods and results. For me, this more than validates these scales.
PTR

As Muslims look at Christians in the Middle East, we feel they are simple and they don't think. We consider ourselves on two sides - we are on one side and they are on the opposite. History tells us of the problems and fights so we have something personally against them.

About Middle Eastern Christians we think that they live better than us, for example we think they love each other and help each other, which is the opposite of us. We think they just follow the West and want to get rid of anything Arabic or Islamic. It seems like this place [the Middle East] is for Arabs and Christians just came to bring Western culture to us.

But Western Christians are very far from us - we look at them as if they want to steal us, control us... very different. Because Christianity is bad and not logical we see that a lot of people in the West have turned away from God. This is because Christianity is unworthy religion. MAX

Scales and the Middle East

When discussing these scales we realised that there are very different perceptions of Christians in the Middle East and the West. Those differences affect how we approach communicating the Gospel. For example in the Middle East the general perception, what is talked about on the street is that Christians are bad. If you asked people in the West, I believe they would not say that, I believe they would probably say 'Christians are boring'. Anti-Christian reactions are a form of interaction, whereas we don't even bother with boring. The Arabs have a proverb to express this, 'Nobody bothers to kick a dead cat!'

There is a need to change the perceptions about followers of Jesus in both the Middle East and the West. The truth is that Christians are not all bad people, nor are they all boring people. However, there is also some truth that Christians are bad people who are saved by God's grace and some Christians are boring people. When there is an element of truth in an accusation it is more difficult to cope with than when it is an outright lie.

Some of the reasons for these perceptions are related to inaccurate perceptions about God, the Church and Mankind. These inaccurate perceptions are both within and outside the church. This is particularly relevant in relationship to the Cultural contextualisation scale. However, it can also be a stumbling block to someone in their journey along the Anti-Christianity to Jesus-follower scale. See the chapter on creativity about the issue of Christians being boring.

With any scale there is almost an implied desire for someone to progress as quickly as possible. We forget that the scale is an indicator of a journey, not a measure of Holiness. So in reading the Anti-Christianity to Jesus-follower scale we should also keep in mind the orientation or direction of the person or the media. For instance, using the scale, someone could be at E -5 but heading towards E -4, or a media item could be at E -3 but cause someone to feel that they should go to E -5. This orientation cannot be shown in the scale but is very important to someone on a spiritual journey.

Anti-Christianity to Jesus-follower scale

The 'Anti-Christianity to Jesus-follower scale' we have used E numbering similar to the Engel scale, but whereas

Engel goes from -8 to +5 we go from -7 to +5. We see this scale as representing the steps or circles in the combined process/ orientation model.

Our scale was created in consultation with a Muslim Background Believer who had no direct reference to the original Engel scale. I merely explained the principles to him and asked him to create a scale that was relevant to his situation. Comparing the two side by side I am amazed by the similarities of the scales, though our scale makes a lot more sense in our situation.

Engel doesn't really fit the vitriolic anti-Christianity person into his scale, someone who is actively working against the Gospel. However, it is probably true that the person has 'initial awareness of the Gospel' even if that awareness is totally inaccurate.

This should be seen as a guide to help us rather than a method of judging people – beginning of Matthew 7 *'Do not judge, or you too will be judged. For in the same way you judge others, you will be judged, and with the measure you use, it will be measured to you.'*

When you read through and look at this scale you might disagree with the numbers we have placed on the scale, depending on your theology you might want to slide the scale down or maybe even up. We ourselves are less worried about the actual position than we are about the orientation of a person and therefore whether they are moving closer to God in their life or moving further away.

Please think of the numbers as labels rather than accurate perceptions of the spiritual position of a person. I am sure that God doesn't think in terms of E numbers, but in terms of His love for us. We use these labels to help us evaluate how appropriate a programme, website or other media tool might be for groups of people with whom we are building or want to build relationships.

It might appear that this progression is blindingly obvious and there is nothing new in it. In a sense this is true, we all know from experience that people rarely if ever jump from being antagonistic towards the Gospel to being a sold out follower of Jesus overnight. Again the purpose of the scale is to help us in evaluating media or programmes to determine how appropriate they might be for a specific group of people.

We see morals as following the law. The government creates laws and controls everything but if the government allows people to lead lives as they would wish then people will be very bad. And because the government doesn't have strict laws in the West this is why morals are bad.

This is popular thought; of course the government or official line is different from this. But, for example, al Jazeera TV says these things very loudly. In some ways we don't consider Middle Eastern Christians not to be Arabic, but we do think they have rejected Arabic culture. It's almost impossible for Muslims to think of Middle Eastern Christians as being truly Arabic. MAX

Maybe the most profitable outcome will be for media producers to grapple with the concepts and edit the scales to their views. Do the process, not just 'buy the T-shirt'. PTR

E7 - you can say they are totally negative. They are very dangerous and violent. You can imagine anything from them. It's a small number of people like this. But they have a big effect and power over the people.

We can just pray for them - we must show them that we are not here for a bad purpose. We can use the general advertisement to say we promote freedom of belief... freedom of speech.

Avoid talking to people when in the presence of such people. They are just totally negative. They say 'Even if they are right and we are wrong... we are still against them'.

The 'war on terror' just increased their anger as it proves their points and gives them more power among the people. They use this as evidence that they are right. 'You see how they treat us'. Showing the opposite - love and patience is the only possible way to win them.

They are very dangerous and strong, but sometimes you find they are very honest [more so than Muslims who might appear more open]. You might be surprised how one word would make a big difference. The right word might take them from E -7 to E4 in one step! You can look at them as sick people who need medicine. MAX

Steps E -7 to E 5

At the start of the scale [E -7] we have someone who is anti-Christianity. Note that we don't say the person is anti-Jesus, but antagonistic towards Christianity. Someone at this point on the scale will be actively fighting against Christians and all that they stand for. If something bad happens to Christians they will express joy at that. They might be actively going around looking for people who are sharing about Jesus either to physically or verbally attack them or to warn others about the dangers these people are expressing. They will be feeling hatred towards Christians and the Church. Fundamentalist Muslims would fall into this category. Paul/Saul started out like this and yet became one of the most effective evangelists of the early church.

With someone so stridently against Christianity you might wonder what we or God can do. For people like this we should be praying that God will soften their heart. Our role is to show love and forgiveness towards them. As Jesus commended us: Love our enemies and pray for those who persecute us[1]. We should 'turn the other cheek'[2]. Direct evangelism is likely to be pointless and counter productive, reinforcing their perceptions of Christianity. Being forthright and standing up to them will also reinforce their feelings towards us rather than bring respect. Indeed, any form of power conflict will likely add fuel to the fire and help them to win converts to their cause.

It is one step up to E -6 where someone would entirely reject Christianity and anything Christian, but without fighting about it. Someone at this position would disagree, often vigorously disagree but show respect to the other person. They might refuse to listen to anything Christian and blame others or castigate others for following Jesus or listening to the message but they would not fight about it.

For someone like this we still want to pray that God will soften their heart, but we can show interest in them, become friends and focus on our similarities rather any differences. Pointing out differences or attempting to communicate any errors in their logic is likely as not to move them to E -7 on the scale rather than produce any helpful result.

The next step would be someone who is neutral and we allocate E -5 to this position. Someone here would allow others

1 Matthew 5:43-48
2 Matthew 5:38-40

to listen to the message, while remaining cold towards Jesus-followers themselves. They might use words like 'Everything is too complex...' or 'I don't want a headache...' or 'I don't care...' What they are expressing is a comfort with the status quo and no desire to look at any form of change. With someone like that we should be looking for the key to communicate the love of God with them and pray that God will make His words burn in their heart.

From being neutral, we step up to someone who is open to the Gospel at E -4. We should encourage that openness and show kindness towards them, showing in our words and deeds the unrelenting love God has for them. As we pray that they will begin to see the truth, they might express what they are hearing as being new and interesting. They will feel that they are free to choose what they believe and follow and will express thoughts like, 'I won't lose anything if I hear you out...' or if someone is trying to silence a Jesus-follower, might say 'Let him speak'.

In a sense we have turned the corner when we get to E -3 where someone is beginning to show interest in Jesus. Someone here has started searching and will begin to ask questions. This is the first stage that we should offer a Bible. They are interested enough to read, and questioning enough to look for themselves. We should pray that the Lord will open their eyes to the importance of Jesus and His message.

We called E -2 the 'maybe' person. Someone who is thinking maybe there is another way. Someone here is more interested in finding God than in what it is called. They are seeking God and 'so long as I get to God' that is the main thing. We should attempt to build bridges with the person, find points of contact and share the Messiah in an open and free way. While we are being open and free, we should pray to God that He will challenge them with the truth about Himself.

At E -1 a person is at the crossroads. They have doubts about themselves and are seriously thinking about the Messiah. They want to know what is the truth and will be asking many questions to which they seriously want answers. At this point we should answer those serious questions, showing evidence and having logical answers. Our Lord said He was the way the truth and the life, so we pray to Him to show them the truth.

When they have passed the crossroads we give them an E 0 position. They may have accepted the truth about the Messiah, but will have questions about what this means for them, their

I'm wary to say this is the first stage we should offer people a Bible. There have been people at E-7 who have read the Bible and God has worked through it to change their views. But also, offering or trying to give a Bible can been seen as trying to be pushy and end up pushing people further away, and becoming more antagonistic if they are only E -4 or -5. Partly this is where model's can't work. People are all individuals. But, fair enough, 'at what stage to offer a Bible' is a good point to think about. DAN

I'm not so happy with the progression terminology here. Maybe add some mention of it not being one-way, I dunno. I know people who as soon as they met Jesus, began telling others about Him all the time, even if they knew virtually nothing about Him. Also people who went from very overt to very private, and others who go from very serious to not really.

I mean, to some degree we go back and forth... Also on E+3, 'enjoy fellowship with other believers' --- not if they live in secret. Or not if the other Christians in the area are all jerks. Or if they just don't fit in.

I think I was somewhere around E+3 or E+4 for a while about 4 years ago, but just didn't fit into the church here, and avoided youth group and so on because I didn't enjoy fellowship with them, and didn't like or want to be within the context of the church. How does being Pro-Jesus Anti-Christian fit in? Dan Kimball's book title: 'They like Jesus, but not the church'. DAN

For me, obeying the 'Great Commission' is discipling others. E5 is thus an integral step in fulfilling that commission.
PTR

family and the community they live in. It's important here to show real care for them. We spend time with them, remaining alongside them.

The worst I heard about what not to do was from someone in Egypt who had up till this point phoned his friend at least once every day. As soon as that person accepted the Messiah as their Lord, the phone calls ceased. When the very hurt friend did make contact with this person, he explained that there were 16 more on his list and that he was number 17, he was therefore concentrating on the other 16. To which the friend replied 'OK, then stop calling me Ashraf [not his real name] just call me 17 instead.'

When they move on from there to E +1, they have moved from acceptance to a decision to follow Jesus. At this point their faith is secret and something internal. We need to encourage them to put their trust in the Messiah into practice as well as theory. We pray the Lord will reassure them of His reality in their heart and that He will meet their needs as they take the next step.

As they express a desire to grow we move them to E +2. They will appear thirsty or hungry for more of the Lord. They will study the Bible on their own, maybe even daily. We should focus on this hunger for the Bible and study it with them. We should aim to introduce them to community meetings of other followers. We pray the Lord will encourage them and specifically overcome any fears they might have in meeting with others.

When they become what we might call a serious follower we might categorize the position as E +3. By now they will enjoy fellowship with other followers, are living out their faith, but maybe still have some reservations.

When God starts challenging them more they will move on to E 4. They are sold out on Jesus, only Jesus, but still within the context of the church. They might consider going on a Discipleship Training Course or some other such course to help them in their walk with the Lord.

The final step we allocated was E +5, where someone has moved on to sharing Jesus with others. There will be observable changes in their life and they will take every chance they have to share Jesus with other people. We need to stand alongside such people, either to learn from them or to encourage them and pray that God will open more doors for them to share the Good News with others.

Clearly not everyone goes through the steps in order. Paul

the Apostle, for example, went from E-7 to E5 almost in one step!

If you prefer, like me, to see things in a diagram rather than words, the following table may help you to see what we mean.

	Description	Signs	God doing	Man's part
E -7	**Anti-Christianity** [& Fighting]	* Jokes, happy with bad news about Christians * Searches out people sharing Jesus (to warn others) * Feelings of hate	* Soften heart	* Turn other cheek * Show love * Show forgiveness
E -6	**Reject** [without fighting]	* Disagrees but shows respect * Refuse to listen * Blame others for changing/listening but not fight about it		* Attract interest * Be friends * Not focus on differences
E -5	**Neutral**	* "Everything complex..." * "Don't want a headache" * "I don't care" * Allows others to listen * Cold to Jesus-followers	* Make words burn inside	* Looking for the key
E -4	**Open**	* "Won't loose anything if I hear" * "Let him speak" * Free to choose * New and interesting	* Begin to see the truth	* Encourage openness * Show kindness
E -3	**Interested** [head knowledge]	* Asks questions * Searching	* Open eyes to importance	* Offer Bible
E -2	**Maybe** [possibly another way]	* "Whatever the way to God... I am interested" * "So long as I get to God"	* Challenging	* Share Jesus in open way * Build bridges
E -1	***Cross-roads*** [doubts and seriously thinking]	* Want to know the truth * Many questions & want answers	* Convincing of truth	* Evidence for truth * Logical sharing
E 0	**Accept** [but reticent]	* "What about my family?" * "What about my community?"		* Be alongside * Don't leave alone
E +1	**Decide to follow Jesus** [internal only]	* Convinced about Jesus but no change, no action * Secret faith	* Reassuring	* [practice as well as theory]
E +2	**Desire to grow**	* Thirsty & hungry to know, asks questions * Meets with others * Reads Bible daily	* Encouraging	* Bible study * Community meetings
E +3	**Serious follower**	* Enjoys fellowship * Live the faith * Not something special in my life * 'Sunday only' follower		
E +4	***Only* Jesus** [but within church]	* Dedicated to Jesus * DTS?	* Challenging	
E +5	**Evangelism**	* Sharing Jesus with others * Observable changes in life * Takes every chance	* Opens doors to share	* Stand beside

Cultural contextualisation scale

There are some Muslims who are seeking after God, and I was one of them. When I became a follower of Jesus it was not converting but felt like returning to my original family. In that sense there are so many aspects of Arabic or Islamic culture that are not negative but positive and from God and I want to keep them and be follower of Jesus in my culture.

If anyone says, 'You have converted or you have changed' my reaction is one of sadness because this is not my feeling. I am the same – I have not changed, I have corrected my way and am now a follower of the true way. I never left my place or my people... I know now who I worship and I am sure of Him.

If someone converts it seems like someone has left his family and gone to join the enemy. No I have not joined the enemy, no I am still one of you, I have just corrected my way. MAX

One of the problems of looking at the Bible is that we do so through coloured glasses. By that I mean if we wear dark maroon sunglasses the world will look dark maroon. It is the same sort of thing reading the Bible. We interpret the Bible through our filter of culture and world view. If we come from a Calvinist or Arminian, Orthodox or Catholic background we will read the Bible with those perceptions. Jesus' words about giving Peter the keys to the church will mean radically different things to a Catholic or a Reformed Presbyterian. The same words in the Bible can end up meaning different things to different people.

These communication difficulties arise from trying to communicate within the Body of Christ. As soon as we add an extra layer of someone being outside the Body and of being from a different culture, the problems multiply till even the simplest form of communication appears to be a major miracle!

Contextualisation is just a word we use to mean putting something into context. Our culture is to some degree helpful and to some degree a hindrance in our relationship with God. It is not neutral. Our culture is the way we express our relationship to others. There is no such thing as a neutral culture and although there are similarities between gatherings of God's people worldwide there are also vast differences. We have over the years contextualised our expression of these gatherings.

In each country there is usually also a Christian sub-culture. Depending on the reaction of the host culture, that Christian sub-culture can be either similar, diametrically opposed to the host culture, or somewhere in between. In countries where the Christian sub-culture is highly dissimilar to the host culture there can be many problems for national believers communicating the Gospel with their neighbours and in new followers of Jesus assimilating into the local expression of the Body of Christ.

Added to this, in places where the Christian church is persecuted by the host culture, there can be a lack of incentive for the church to reach out to those who are persecuting them.

When groups of Jesus-followers from a Muslim host culture wish to meet together as some sort of expression of the gathering of the Body of Christ, they can be faced with two problems. They face either rejection or alienation by the host culture and/or rejection or alienation by the Christian sub-culture. There is a tendency either to remain secret believers with no linkage to the wider Body of Christ, or to totally throw off their background and embrace the Christian sub-culture. If they embrace the Christian sub-culture it makes it difficult for them to reconnect or share their faith with their friends and neighbours.

When we look at Jesus calling us to be salt and light within the community, embracing a sub-culture makes this close to impossible. Taking Jesus' metaphor of him being the vine[1] or a tree and us being the branches, and Paul's metaphor of branches grafted into the tree[2], we can extend this to think about the world view and characteristics of someone who is a Christian.

In Cyprus we have many citrus groves, and I am told that you must graft a sweet orange tree branch onto good and bitter orange tree root stock. As you walk along the streets you can see many orange trees in the pavement. It's not uncommon for tourists to pick surreptitiously [they think they are doing wrong] an orange from one of these trees. When they peel and eat this orange they are shocked to find the orange dreadfully bitter. The trees along the sides of the roads are there for shade, the oranges are not for eating.

Now if you look at the leaves on one the branches of these bitter orange trees and compare them with the leaves on one of the branches of a grafted sweet orange tree, you would be hard pushed to know the difference. The fruit, on the other hand, are very different. So it is when we are grafted into the Lord. The leaves may look similar but the fruit is different. We are totally grafted into a new world view, a new root stock.

In our enthusiasm for getting rid of the old life we often confuse new Christians. For instance, a friend of mine from a Buddhist background was encouraged to cast off all the Buddhist practices. He lent me a book of Buddhist practices. Consider this:

> *Parents must re-evaluate their priorities. It has become fashionable for parents to compare the academic achievements of their children with other parents. By all means encourage the child to excel in his studies, but a child should not be evaluated only*

In some places its more serious than that. If someone wishes to continue breathing then becoming disconnected from their culture can be dangerous. We know that for many people from a Muslim background martyrdom is very real. PTR

1 John 15:1-4
2 Romans 11:17-25

> *on the basis of his academic achievement. We must accept him for what he is, and not what we expect him to be.*[1]

Motivation should be changed when someone becomes a Christian, but we should be careful not to reject and cast off 'leaves' just because they came from the old tree. It's not true that a Buddhist becoming a follower of Jesus should now start to evaluate his children purely on academic achievement, merely to be the opposite of Buddhism! The same is true for Muslims who decide to follow Jesus. They have changed the person to whom they are connected; they are now part of a new root stock. This does not mean they must necessarily throw aside ***all*** their previous beliefs and practices.

It appears to me that in the Middle East, 'Christian' culture is significantly affected by Islamic culture. However, in some ways it is more affected by an inaccurate perception of the church. When we say the word church, whether in the Middle East or west, there is a strong linkage to two things: a meeting and a meeting place. The meeting is often the Sunday or Friday service and the place a building dedicated to that meeting.

I think this could be offensive to some people. It seems to me that the survival/ghetto mentality, within the context of the increasing Islamisation of the region, it is not very surprising! However, their model of church does tend to be very Old Testament - like the Jews - where they feel they are called out to form an 'other' culture. We need to see a reformation and the real message of Jesus for all nations.
PTR

Evangelical Christians spend a lot of time saying, 'The church is people not the building.' There is truth in that, but there is still a significant over-emphasis on a congregation-based model for church. Maybe it is not the building, but they do see it primarily as the group with whom they meet regularly.

People who share the love of Jesus with others all around the world have developed what is called a 'contextualisation index'. This is a scale that shows how closely an expression of the Body of Christ is linked into or alien to the host culture. In order to help us in our communication, we have taken that scale and modified it to our region of the Middle East.

At one end of the scale we have an expression of the church that is alien to the host culture and we give this the number C1. At the other end we have a secret believer, who is totally at one with the host culture and alienated from what appears to them to be a very distant Christian church. We give this the index C5.

In between these two extremes we have a continuum - C2, C3, and C4 have each also been given labels of: Informal church meeting, home meeting and group meeting. Because

1 How to live without Fear and Worry, Dr K Sri Dhammananda, page 227

many of us have been to meetings with these names we tend to associate our expectations with those experiences. This can be unhelpful in trying to understand this index.

All parts of the contextualisation scale are expressions of the church, from the secret believer to the open Sunday congregation. In no way is this scale a progression or journey. Any number of secret believers are still as much a part of the church as the most lively Sunday church congregation. There is no right or wrong; each have benefits and drawbacks.

In order to help us evaluate media for use in different contexts, with the help of a Muslim Background Believer, we then added different observable phenomena. Although we talk about a continuum, often the phenomena have discrete steps. For example, we see no singing expressed as an appropriate part of a meeting until C2, an informal church meeting (see page 47 for a table).

The way to see this index is more of a continuum than the table suggests. This is not an accurate measured table, it is a set of guidelines to help in placement of a radio or tv programme, website or other media tool into its context. For example, singing is very alien to a Muslim expression of worship, fitting more into the setting of an immoral nightclub; so coming to a Christian church and seeing people singing would be mind-blowing to a conservative Muslim who has decided to follow Jesus. So for something that is contextualised to the degree of C3-C5 it would be inappropriate to have any singing.

Décor is also of special significance. Crosses and icons and statues of saints could be seen as blasphemous to a Muslim; and so when someone decides to follow Jesus this can be a big problem in seeing these as a freedom. This is similar to the problem Paul talked about with respect to food dedicated to idols. Hence when considering décor, the cross is not introduced till you get to C1; it might bear thinking about how the fish symbol was used by the early church as a secret icon to identify a family or individual as a follower of Christ and that the cross was not used openly during that period.

We should note that this scale shows what is possible culturally rather than what is necessarily desirable. The question of whether didactic or dialectic communication is better, more effective or 'right' is not addressed in these scales. The central question is how alien or acceptable an activity would feel for someone from a Muslim background along a continuum to a 'normal' Christian church.

Personally I think that something in the middle of the range

Arabic is something heavenly, something high. Because in paradise they speak Arabic, because the prophet Mohammed spoke Arabic, the Qu'ran is in Arabic... we want the whole world to speak Arabic. There is something much deeper than just the language.

The Christians have a Bible that is not Arabic... the names are not Arabic... so when the Bible is translated into Arabic we see it as just a language, not this deep embedded meaning. In Egypt they say, 'Even the land speaks Arabic'. As a Muslim I could not imagine God speaking English... yes, He understands it, but I must speak in Classical Arabic to speak to God in His language.

Culture is very important for Arabs. We look at the first Arabs as great people. MAX

is probably helpful, in that as a secret believer it is difficult to have any form of realistic fellowship, while at the other extreme, a church that is totally alien to it's host culture will find it difficult to reach out to others.

So, although everyone on the scale is part of the Body of Christ, there are problems with the extremes. Someone at C5, a secret believer, will not have any real fellowship other than possibly one on one with a few other followers. Jesus promised that where two or three are gathered, He is there in the midst of them. So a gathering as small as two is a legitimate expression of the Body of Christ. In some situations it is necessary to be a secret believer, but it's desirable that someone is not forced by circumstances to be restricted in that gathering.

By contrast, a church at C1 is likely to feel alien to people from a Muslim background. Some of the things we in the west find normal would be shocking. I remember talking to one believer and one of the things he found shocking was the singing. Singing is not something done in praise of God in Islam, yet in different forms is common in almost every Christian church. A church at C1, or media projects that appear to be very C1 in outlook are going to find great difficulty in communicating the gospel to Musilms

Personally, even as someone from the west who has grown up all my life in the church, I find the C3 expression of the body of Christ closer to what I see Jesus advocating and the early church practicing. I know for many, however, that the Sunday morning gathering is something they feel is a key part of their Christian life.

Whatever our church background, encouraging development of house fellowships within the context of gatherings of Muslim background believers is unlikely to do any harm. The important thing is not to make it appear that either a C1 expression of the church is the most desirable, or that others are somehow inferior.

In North America, Africa and Korea there is another expression of church that is gaining favour, the so called 'mega-church'. Thousands, and sometimes tens of thousands of people gather together to praise God and then listen to one person deliver a talk. Often these mega-churches have some form of small-group structure beneath them. In our 20th and 21st century idea of 'bigger is better', these churches have immense appeal to some people. Some of these mega-churches even have shopping malls and villages/townships for

Here's my experience as someone who was a Muslim. When I met a Christian he invited me to meet other Christian people but I refused. I refused because it was too dangerous for me to meet in open with Christians.

Then I was asked to join a group of other Christians who had been followers of Islam. I would not join a group like this either. Why? I feel I cannot bind my destiny to somebody else.

For me the best is meeting with followers of Jesus from my background but from other towns - this is much safer. I am more comfortable if people are strangers.
MAX

their members.

This appears to me to be almost a C0 expression of culture; they are no longer salt and light within the community as Jesus commissioned us to be but totally separate. There are other churches, like some of the Brethren, the Amish and others who have also been separatist. These are not included in the diagram below, but seeing them as the logical end of the spectrum will help us to realise some of the potential pitfalls of that end of the continuum.

As far as media to share the love of God with Muslims goes, C0 is so unhelpful as to be not worth considering. The idea of an isolated mega-church within the Arab world is so alien and so frightening in the message it conveyed that people would see that I believe it should never be considered.

The following table shows the sort of phenomena that you might see in the various expressions of the body of Christ at different levels of contextualisation. Note, these are not fixed, they are indicative of a level of contextualisation and they help us in evaluating media. They are not right or wrong and since this is the first version of this table it is very much a work in progress.

In churches they might use a few words in another language, Greek, English, French, but in a mosque you cannot use anything other than classical Arabic. MAX

	C5	C4	C3	C2	C1
	Secret believer	**Group meeting**	**Home meeting**	**Informal 'Church Meeting'**	**Sunday Church & other activities**
Speaker	One-on-one	Leader gives talk	Discussion	Short preaching	Preaching
Men/Women	Separate	Separate	Mixed in family	Mixed	Mixed
Location	Coffee shop/home	Sitting on floor	Sitting on chairs	Sitting on chairs	Church (pews/chairs
Prayer	One-on-one	Only leader prays	Pray for each other	Prayer	Open prayer
Meal	Coffee/Juice No pork	No meal	Meal but no pork, no alcohol	Meal but no pork, no alcohol	Pork? Alcohol?
Singing	No singing	No singing	No singing	Singing	Singing
Dancing	No dancing	No dancing	No dancing	No dancing	Dancing
Décor	No cross No icons	No cross No icons Scripture verse pictures	No cross No icons Scripture verse pictures	No cross No icons Scripture verse pictures	Cross Icons Statues (as appropriate)
Subjects	No controversial issues		Focus on relationships		Apologetics Any subjects
Language	Normal words and expressions	Normal words and expressions	Some Christian phrases (but explained)	Some Christian phrases (but explained)	Christian expressions

In this scale we have focussed on the external aspects of contextualisation - what we can see - which is particularly relevant to evaluating programme materials. However, alongside this, identity and community are critical. As Bob Goldmann puts it 'the *identity* that new believers choose and the way they interact with their *community* will have a great effect on whether others from their culture will make a similar choice to follow Jesus'[1].

Cultural contextualisation can be different from what Goldmann calls 'full contextualisation'. For instance, while following external cultural patterns it is possible for new believers to adopt an identity that others from their community perceive to be foreign or associate with other believers in a way that their community perceive to be extracted from that community.

About Middle Eastern Christians - to be Arabic, you have to prove it. They speak a different language. What is the evidence that you are Arabic? Maybe they are Arab, but another type of Arab...

For instance, for someone from the UK and the English language... it is just a language... if you don't use English but another language... do you feel guilty? Do you feel you have betrayed your people?

But for Arabic Muslims there is something more. There is a special relationship between Arabic and Islam.
MAX

If we wish to be salt and light ***within*** our communities, we need to ***remain within*** them. That may sound obvious, but it often requires us to go further than merely observing external aspects of the culture, to remain integrated with the community from which we come. This isn't easy. Historically, Christians have swung like a pendulum from one extreme to the other.

In a sense we should not think so much about contextualisation, but about incarnation. When Jesus became man he was what we call incarnate: God in flesh. He was still God, but He took on the likeness of man to the degree he felt what we felt and suffered as we suffer, and was part of a community. Although we talk about contextualisation then, our real aim is incarnation.

When we incarnate the Gospel, people perceive it to be natural to their culture. Bob Goldmann created the table[2] shown on the next page to show the contrast.

1 Mission Frontiers, September-October 2006: Are we accelerating or inhibiting movements to Christ? Bob Goldmann, page 9
2 Mission Frontiers, September-October 2006: Are we accelerating or inhibiting movements to Christ? Bob Goldmann, page 10

Identity	
Preserve an Insider Identity as Believers	**Establish a Foreign Identity as Believers**
◆ Gospel is perceived as "inside", "natural" to their culture.	◆ Gospel is perceived as "foreign", "outside" to their culture.
◆ New believers are encouraged to preserve an identity that will allow them to reach their families and communities with the gospel (rather than being expelled because they converted to a foreign religion).	◆ New believers identify themselves as Christians, and are understood to have left their ethno-religious culture.
◆ New believers remain in their culture. If that culture is strongly intertwined with religion, then believers are free to follow Jesus while remaining "inside" their ethno-religious identity. (eg "I'm a Muslim who follows Jesus", rather than "I've converted to Christianity to follow Jesus.")	◆ New believers are expelled by their family or community, or are coerced into abandoning their new faith, because they've chosen to convert to a foreign religion.

The phrase '*I'm a Muslim who follows Jesus*' will ring alarm bells to many people, being concerned about syncretism: That is, creating a new religion that is a mixture of Christianity and Islam. This is a real fear and one that needs to be considered whenever we look at the question of contextualisation. However, we should not see this in isolation, assuming it is only related to our reaching out to others. It might be a sobering thought to consider to what extent what we think of as Christianity is in reality a syncretism of Christianity and western modernism and materialism.

There is no easy answer to this dilemma. It is something we have to continually watch and bring before the Lord as we seek to reach others with the Gospel.

Boldness scale

The Boldness scale may be another valuable tool for working out where any particular piece of communication can be placed. But it would be dangerous if all the communication took place within one section. We are and should be salt and light in the world. Being in the world means being integrated into everyday life. That means that a discussion about football could be as important as a discussion about the Lordship of Jesus in helping someone along their journey of faith. The person who is always only talking about Jesus might be salt and light, but they are not in the world and they are, as I believe the Western perception of Christians is... boring!

It is important to be integrated people and it's important that our media is also integrated. One of the websites we host and are involved with has a secular news feed on it. The news feed is not there merely as a hook to draw people in, but to allow the site to be integrated into daily life.

Remember this scale was developed by us for evaluating media. Though it may be usable in other contexts of sharing the gospel, it was not intended for that. It is therefore not a scale to encourage Bible-bashing, as if the bolder we are the better. Rather, it's a way of seeing how different programmes, web-sites, etc, fit into the overall scheme of sharing the Good News of the Messiah.

Our scale here starts at B1, where communication can be about anything. In spiritual terms the content is not important at all. It can be about sport, weather, politics... anything. Nobody here would have any idea that you were interesting in anything spiritual, let alone Christian.

At B2, the communication is about normal friendly communication topics, demonstrating an open-heart and trust.

At B3, the communication is about important life topics, but not religious topics. It would include subjects like family, health, society... someone would believe you to be a caring person, but would not realise any spiritual side to your life.

At B4, the communication is about God in general. This is the first step in any form of spiritual communication, but with ambiguity. Topics such as God's mercy, his love, his generosity might be included here.

B5 is where we first introduce Jesus. We might compare texts from the Qu'ran and the Bible or just show or quote references from the Bible. This is done in a neutral noninvasive way.

B6 takes us to the personal importance of Jesus in our lives. Expressions of the greatness of Jesus and the miracles He performed would be included.

B7 is a clear expression of the gospel, for us, and would include the concept of sin, salvation and that Jesus is Lord of our lives.

B8 is the final step in this scale, not just expressing Jesus is Lord for us, but that it is important for everyone. People are challenged with a choice, Jesus is the only way, and without Him we are lost.

There are two things that we have observed. Firstly, that some people focus on what they might call pre-evangelism and we would call B3/B4. There is nothing wrong with this, but there are two dangers: In terms of the process model, this can help a person on their pilgrimage towards God, but it's important to be integrated into something that helps them move on. B3/B4 isolated communication can end up encouraging someone to feel that what they believe is all that is needed.

The second thing we have observed is that some people who are trying to reach Muslims focus exclusively on B8. This can be seen by Muslims as antagonistic. There are few people who have developed programmes that take account of a person's development of understanding about the Messiah. A progressive approach to boldly proclaiming the gospel is more likely to bear fruit, as it is closer to what we see Jesus doing while he was on earth.

The following table shows the steps in a diagrammatic form.

	Content	Examples
B1	Anything/not important at all	* Sport * Weather * Politics * Problems
B2	Relationships, build friendship	* Things that make people trust you * Encourage open-heart
B3	Deeper topics, but not religious,	* Family * Health * Society * Caring
B4	Talking about God in general	* Mercy * Love * Generosity
B5	Special position of Jesus, God & Jesus	* Introduce Bible * Show Jesus in Qu'ran/Bible
B6	Importance of Jesus in our lives	* Talk direct about Jesus as great person * Miracles (still today)
B7	Jesus is Lord	* Jesus as Lord * Why miracles? * Sin * Adam * Salvation
B8	You **must** accept Jesus as Lord	* You have to chose * Only way * Lost without Him

Culture, counter culture and alternative culture

When we talk about contextualisation we mean the relationship between followers of Jesus and the 'host culture' - in other words the context of the Gospel in the surrounding culture.

Jesus expresses this relationship in terms of salt and light.

> *You are salt for the earth. But if salt loses its taste, how will it be made salty again? It is no longer good for anything except to be thrown out and trampled on by people. You are light for the world. A city cannot be hidden when it is located on a hill. No one lights a lamp and puts it under a basket. Instead, everyone who lights a lamp puts it on a lamp stand. Then its light shines on everyone in the house. In the same way let your light shine in front of people. Then they will see the good that you do and praise your Father in heaven.*[1]

When Jesus said this, it may have appeared to be something new to His listeners. However, in reality it was just restating what God had said down through the ages, starting from Abraham. And right down through the ages the people of God have become distracted and not been salt and light within the community and culture. They have built an alternative culture and community instead.

Going right back to the beginning, when God spoke to Abraham He said:

> *My promise is still with you. You will become the father of many nations. So your name will no longer be Abram, but Abraham because I have made you a father of many nations... I will make my promise to you and your descendants for generations to come as an everlasting promise. I will be your God and the God of your descendants.*[2]

1 Matthew 5:13-16
2 Genesis 17:4-7

In the Middle East names have meanings - Abram means 'exalted father' and his new name Abraham means 'father of many'. Yet the people of God seemed to miss the emphasis on being God's emissary to many nations and focussed on verse 8. I deliberately stopped at verse 7 to show the emphasis. Verse 8 says: *I am also giving this land where you are living- all of Canaan-to you and your descendants as your permanent possession. And I will be your God.* Sadly, God's people, as they have throughout the ages, have focussed on the separate alternative community rather than the integrated relationship to the many.

In Middle East, church is hidden, not really seen in the society or culture at all. If there is a Christian group [from a Muslim background] in my town, they will meet in secret and nobody will know about them. They meet to pray and they go through society and talk on an individual level - talk with friends about what they believe.

The appearance of the city is very important. They can have an influence on the city, but they cannot have a separate personality or culture. Even westerners who come here have to live like us. MAX

Frequently Christians form some sort of parallel, alternative culture to the host culture and it is observed that this alternative culture tends to inhibit the spread of the Gospel into the host culture. This is because when there is a second parallel alternative culture, the Gospel is seen as foreign or alien, not something that is 'for me'.

There are other problems with this alternative culture. One of the most significant is that when members of the alternative culture find all their needs met within this community, they can become progressively more isolated from their host culture. This isolation, over time, makes the host culture seem something undesirable, and communication with members of the other community tends to become merely functional - buying, selling and working alongside them but without real communication or understanding. As this isolation increases, so the appearance of this alternative culture becomes more and more strange and alien to members of the host culture. This makes it progressively more difficult for members of the host culture to cross over into the alternative culture and evangelism diminishes until the alternative culture goes into survival mode with no real desire for meaningful contact with the host culture. This is roughly what could be seen from Christian communities in the Middle East up to the mid 1990s. However, like all generalisations, there were exceptions.

Over time, the language of the alternative culture can change. Christians start to use words and phrases that are meaningful to them, but ambiguous or incomprehensible to members of the host culture. This can happen both ways and the host culture - especially among the young - can adopt a way of speaking that the Christians don't commonly use. Sometimes the Christians might attempt to emulate this language. But without understanding properly the culture, these attempts can seem 'pseudo' to the host culture and actually be counter productive in communicating the Gospel.

Sometimes the separation is quite deliberate on the part of the Christians. This was the case for the Puritans who were the founding fathers of the USA. They were having difficulties within the culture of the established churches in Europe and hoped to found a new and free culture where they could practice their faith without interference. Though some native Americans became followers of Jesus, the alternative culture had little meaningful contact with their host culture. The pendulum has swung right across now, with 'megachurches' setting up alternative communities right across the USA . In *Branded Nation: The Marketing of Megachurch, College Inc.*, and Museumworld, James B. Twitchell gives the example of Southeast Christian in Louisville, Kentucky:

> *Southeast Christian is an example of a new breed of megachurch -- a full-service "24/7" sprawling village, which offers many of the conveniences and trappings of secular life wrapped around a spiritual core. It is possible to eat, shop, go to school, bank, work out, scale a rock-climbing wall and pray there, all without leaving the grounds.*
>
> *These churches are becoming civic in a way unimaginable since the 13th century and its cathedral towns. No longer simply places to worship, they have become part resort, part mall, part extended family and part town square.*[1]

The megachurch example may have come out of a desire to contextualize or reach out to a generation that some Church leaders believe are being lost to the Gospel. However, in reaching out, they have not remained salt and light within the host community; rather they have separated themselves entirely. Looking in from the outside it might be questionable whether indeed these alternative communities are syncretistic forms of religion. Wikipedia defines religion as 'a set of common beliefs and practices generally held by a group of people, often codified as prayer, ritual, and religious law'. As such they appear more a form of religion than a relationship with a living God.

1 The Marketing of Megachurch, College Inc., and Museumworld - James B Twitchell

It is worth noting that until Christianity became a state established religion, followers of the Messiah sought to be salt and light within the community rather than changing the entire culture to be what is perceived as Christian.

The Christian alternative culture does not only relate to how people speak. It could affect how they dress, hairstyles, makeup (or lack of it), means of transport (like the Amish) or thousands of other small things that members of the host culture perceive as alternative. We know from experience, for instance, how easily we can spot a Mormon just from the look of their haircut and clothes.

But it isn't just that extreme. Some Christians would be critical of some sub-cultures of the host culture. For instance, in some places, for men a 'clean cut' hairstyle is still considered somehow to be more Christian than long hair - even if among the general population long hair would be acceptable. That is just an example of something obvious. There can be many subtle cultural signs and indicators that members of a community pick up to know if someone is 'one of our people' or a 'foreigner'. Frequently people outside emulate some of the characteristics of the group while missing others. They are inconsistent. That inconsistency is of itself an indicator of being an outsider.

Other Christians, citing the incarnation - God becoming flesh - would see contextualisation as continuing this incarnational approach. Christians feeling this way would see a Biblical mandate to be 'in the world yet not of the world'; to be fully integrated in the world, yet hold a different 'world view' from those around them. For some, the host culture is seen as neutral - neither good nor bad - and following Jesus can be worked out within that context. They might see man as fallen, but emphasise the good and wholesome aspects of the host culture.

However, no culture is perfect, as no culture is 100 percent bad. This applies as much to the Christian alternative cultures as to the host cultures. They too have some good and some bad attributes.

The early followers of Jesus, or followers of the Way as they preferred to be called, thought of themselves as visitors in a foreign country. They were just passing through en route to their heavenly home. People around them where they lived perceived this and accepted them as almost foreigners. It was not until the third century when the Emperor of Rome made Christianity the state religion that it became something

If a church or group of believers in a Muslim city behaves in a different and free way, for instance in the clothes they wear or if, for instance, husbands and wives were seen holding hands this would set up an alternative culture and would therefore have no influence on the culture.

As another example, if a Christian wears a beard, wears modest clothes then we would think of the person as righteous and be surprised that the person is a Christian. 'How come you are a Christian if you are a good man?'

How you look is very important. MAX

normal to be a Christian.

Since then there has always been an ongoing tension. When the followers of Christ were within, but not of the culture they did not exhibit an alternative culture but a counter culture. This difference between an alternative and a counter culture may seem like just playing with words but I think the difference is relevant and significant.

When we talk about an alternative culture we are thinking about something that effectively runs parallel with the host culture and replaces it. Christians are not the only groups who exhibit this alternative culture phenomena - many ethnic and other religious groups also can create alternative cultures within a host culture. This can be significant when trying to reach, for example, Afro-Caribeans living in Birmingham in the UK or Palestinians living in Jordan.

When we think about a counter culture we are not talking about a replacement culture, but a culture integrated into a host culture which nevertheless exhibits characteristics which can be considered to be running counter to the host culture. For example, in a host culture which shows a high level of personal independence like in North America or Western Europe, a counter culture of followers of Jesus might show a high level of inter-dependence.

This separation between alternative and counter culture affects how we think about contextualisation. You might think of counter culture as being lifestyle choices within a host culture. Contextualisation therefore appears natural and part of being counter cultural, whereas it can seem forced or artificial if attempted from an alternative culture.

There are also questions about how this fits in Biblically. For example, within some cultures in the Middle East it is important to look well-dressed and for events to have almost an air of decadence. Being rich is admired. Therefore if a TV preacher looks well dressed in an auditorium that is full of well dressed people who appear to have paid quite a bit of money to be there [even if the truth is the event is free] this alternative culture can create affirmative feelings in the host culture. But Biblically I want to ask the question is this good news for the poor? Good news for the poor is counter culture!

The question this raises is how it affects the three core questions of this book - creativity, dialogue and storytelling as a means of communicating the Gospel to people from the

It's not all right in Muslim culture - if I see someone on the sea front and I see a boy kiss a girl and she doesn't have any direct relationship with him, isn't married for example, then it's very bad and we would go and tell the whole city about her. This would result in nobody being prepared to marry the girl publicly.

We do things wrong in Muslim culture, but always in secret. Appearance is very important.

There are some churches in Muslim cities, but they don't have freedom. They are like a salt container on the table but not added to the food. Many of the churches are empty of people from the locality, they are full of strangers from outside. They come into the city to go to the church, they are not part of the city. MAX

Middle East. The best way of approaching this is to start from the position of a member of the host culture who has just decided to follow the Messiah, but has no experience of an alternative culture. Thinking about the claims and teaching of Jesus will affect their lifestyle which will tend to be counter cultural in places, but entirely different from context to context. It will not necessarily have any linkage with an existing alternative culture.

An example here might help. A group of new Muslim Background Believers might decide to share a meal, pray and study the Bible together on a weekly basis. This meeting might be very different from the Sunday meeting of an established church. This meal together might express a closeness of relationship and caring for each other across what would not normally be their family or tribal groups. It might not involve singing songs, a sermon or other 'church' events while still being a valid expression of 'church'. This then is counter cultural in that it starts from the host culture, is not significantly abnormal within the host culture, but runs counter to the expected family or tribal groupings of the host culture.

I thought that going to church was like going to the mosque... and I met with people who are wonderful believers but they didn't religiously go to church like we went to the mosque. It was hard to not see following the Messiah as a similar religion. MAX

From the point of view of the three core questions of the book, I hope it is clear that we need to start from the host culture and use as creative approach as possible to communicate the Gospel, while remaining in dialogue with the host culture. Storytelling - or using parables - remains an excellent way of communicating, as can be seen by the way Jesus used parables within the context of first century Palestine. Those stories or parables can focus on aspects of the culture that communicate God's truth in a way that transcends culture.

Our danger point that we must always watch and be aware of is that we are called to be salt and light within the community, not a parallel alternative community separated from the host community. When we become separated, then there is a danger that, as Jesus said, the salt will lose its saltiness.

Born again jargon

As I mentioned in the introduction, a friend of mine was talking to a Buddhist about the Gospel and told him that in order to be a Christian he had to be born again. It was a few days later in talking to this same Buddhist that I realised when my friend had said 'born again' he was referring to something spiritual, whereas the Buddhist had heard it as literal. Since he believed in re-incarnation, he thus thought that Christians also believe in re-incarnation.

'Born again' is not a phrase Jesus used repeatedly, but has become a piece of jargon coined by some Christians for them to communicate the need for a new start, a repenting or turning around in direction. However, this phase in itself can cause confusion. Especially to Buddhists. One can see why the early believers were sometimes confused with cannibals, since they 'ate the body and drank the blood' of our Lord Jesus.

We have surrounded ourselves with jargon which means things to us, but not to others. This is not unique to Christianity. My hobby is sailing. For those who know the jargon a halyard, a sheet and an outhaul are all straightforward words on a boat. For the uninitiated they are both confusing and possibly misleading, especially as a sheet is a rope attached to a sail, and not the sail itself, as most non-sailors might have thought.

There is a common perception among some Christians that we should wherever possible use Biblical words and phrases to express spiritual or church concepts, hence the leadership team of a church is often not called that, but is instead called the eldership. I'm not sure if this is more confusing if the people concerned are elderly or young people! The phrase 'born-again' has a similar aura surrounding it. Somehow this phrase, which Jesus may or may not have actually used [the text is ambiguous and could have meant 'born from above'], has come into common Christian phraseology to mean the process of deciding to follow Jesus and/or the change happening to someone when they have been chosen by God to be one of the people to spend eternity with him. And it becomes clumsier and clumsier trying to find sentences to express what it means.

Part of the problem is that these phrases have not been neatly defined. Whereas one person might understand

When I first met Christians they used a lot of jargon. It was Arabic they were speaking but it was very strange. I could not understand the bigger meaning behind the words. I thought that unless I lived with Christians for a long while I would not understand their words. I would have my own faith, but not be able to communicate. MAX

It's like a chain round your neck. Each society has a chain round their neck of words that are special to them. Only by contact can you understand their words. For example even the word 'salvation' – I thought it was like a car to enter paradise. Salvation means something more, but I thought it was fast track to paradise. Also they [Christians] use heaven instead of paradise and I would say 'What about paradise?'

To understand that you are a sinner even if you don't do something obviously wrong in your life... this was a very hard concept to understand. I had tried to live a pure life and so it was hard to understand the Christian concept of a sinner. MAX

I work with people from all over the world, in English, which for most people is a second or third language, and our community is very much a Christian bubble/alternate culture C1/C0 type of place. One very surprised comment I have heard many times is, 'I don't know how to write to Christians in my country and tell them about what life is like, we don't have a word for "Ministry"!' And then they are even more surprised when I tell them it's not a common English word either, and that talking with non-Christian English speakers, they also will not understand - to them, Ministry is something to do with government offices. DAN

There are two Arabics - Islamic Arabic and Christian Arabic and even now, some years later I struggle to understand Christian Arabic. I long to find a way to combine them and not have a barrier between them. I want to make a bridge. If I found a treasure I want to be able to share this with my family. But the language is the barrier to sharing it. Even educated people cannot understand... I feel very strange.

Sometimes I find there is a difference between the language of the Bible and the language of Christian people. And the Bible is easier than the language of the Christian people! MAX

'born again' to be signed up church member, another might understand it to be something spiritual rather than physical. Of course we would all hope that signed up church members have also been accepted by God into His family. But compare this to the parable of the sheep and the goats in the Bible[1], we see a very different story, where even those who have called Him Lord here on earth can be in the group Jesus doesn't own at the time of reckoning.

This problem of confusion over language means that when we look at the process by which someone becomes a follower of Jesus; it is not only ambiguous linguistically but also procedurally. Not that it is ambiguous in either sense for any one person, or even maybe a group of people within the same sub-culture in the church. But it is very ambiguous when trying to communicate across different sub-cultures of the church.

This is further confused by the fact that many of us use phrases which we believe have come from the Bible, when in fact they have come from later interpreters of the Bible. This phrase 'born again' is one such phrase. If you ask the average Christian where the phrase 'born again' comes from in the Bible, they will point to the dialogue between Jesus and Nicodemus, often misquoting 'Unless a man is born again he cannot enter the Kingdom of Heaven'[2]. It doesn't say that. It says 'Unless a man is born of water and the Spirit...' Maybe this is the same thing if you interpret it that way, but one should be careful not to interpret what is not there.

So, in determining whether someone is inside or outside the Kingdom of God, there are a number of things that we should look at from Scripture. What is the Kingdom of God? Is it an inside/outside thing? What did Jesus do when he called people to follow him? What did he commission us to do? All these and other thoughts need to be reconciled if we are to evaluate how and at what step people are at, to provide appropriate media to help them along this path.

A friend of mine who is a missiologist said he preferred the phrase 'the unrelenting power of God to change you is near you' to the 'Kingdom of God'. Certainly the word kingdom is ambiguous. For example, when we say the phrase United Kingdom we think of a country, a divided country made up of three other countries and a province. When I was growing up the phrase 'Kingdom of God' was defined as 'those people in

1 Matthew 25:31-46
2 John 3:3-5

the world who accept the rule of Jesus in their lives'. In some ways that's a good definition, but do we mean they accept it 100%, mostly, sometimes, or that it means 'those people who want to accept the rule of Jesus in their lives when they are not doing the opposite'. I know for myself, I could not say I am 100% of the time accepting the rule of Jesus in my life.

Arabic has two words for Kingdom: Malakoot and Memlekkah. Malakoot refers to the kingdom in the sense 'Kingdom of God' and Memlekkah in the sense 'Kingdom of Saudi Arabia'. English doesn't have that separation of words. Alongside that, Jesus generally said 'the Kingdom of God is near', implying proximity rather than entrance. Thus, 'the unrelenting power of God to change you is near you' makes more sense than 'those people in the world who accept the rule of Jesus in their lives are near to you'.

Even if we accept the definition as being a defined group of people who will spend eternity with God, to what extent can we know whether someone is in or out of that group? The Bible is clear that at some stage in the future there will be a time when the line is drawn. Some will be spending eternity with God and others will not. There is divergence on interpretation of the Bible among Christians, even Christians who base their faith exclusively on the Bible, as to what exactly happens to those who will not. For now, we'll just leave it that some will spend eternity with God and some will not. The time when the line is drawn is either some time in the future or some time in the past.

Even the word 'Christian', is not easily defined. I remember talking with a prominent Christian statistician about this. In *Operation World*[1] they allocate percentages of the major world religions to each country. In that book they use the word Christian by self definition. In other words if someone calls themselves a Christian, then they count as Christian in their statistics. This may be more helpful as a statistical measure than a measure of a person's spiritual orientation. Alongside this we have the problem of whether we have any right to make a judgement about a person's spiritual relationship to God.

The idea of listening to God, hearing him (I had done this before, but it is an alien thought in Islam and I thought I was strange) but then finding this is what God wants when I became a follower of Jesus, this was a big surprise. When I heard someone say 'I want to learn how to listen to God' I thought this strange and it was a big difference to find this was normal.

'Kingdom of God' - Malakoot - means things that He created, there are many things in the Qu'ran that He created, angels, heaven and things like, but He doesn't live there, he is above and beyond that. When we go to paradise we will not live with Him. He is above us and will still be separate from us. There is a big difference - paradise is a place to spend eternity, but not with God. There might be place to meet with Him, but not to live with Him. A lot of groups in Islam don't believe we will even see God on the last day. So the idea is very different.

Even after following the Messiah for some years I still struggle to understand the idea of the Kingdom of God. MAX

1 Operation World - Patrick Johnstone, Jason Mandryk and Robyn Johnstone

Boring?

There's a part of what I do that I love and hate at the same time: Giving talks in church services and other places both excites and makes me feel bad at the same time.

I do enjoy telling people about what I do, because it shows what God is doing in the area. I often tell people how we are just almost running alongside while God is doing things. As an example, we believed God was telling us to start an Internet radio station. To do this we needed money for some expenses and equipment to set up a studio. A group in the UK had offered some money conditional on us acquiring all the rest of what we needed to set up. This was encouraging, but we had no idea where to find the rest. Out of the blue I had a phone call from someone in Europe offering equipment 'What do you need?' he asked. I sent him my 'shopping list' and he said he would provide it and that he had a friend coming to Cyprus who could bring it out.

As we were praying we felt that as well as the studio in Cyprus we should build a studio in Egypt. A studio in Egypt would enable many more people to be involved, but would carry a risk with it. There is no law in Egypt covering Internet broadcasting, so we didn't know if the authorities would close it down within a day, a week, a month or ignore it totally. For that reason we needed a studio in Cyprus as well so that if they did close it down we could continue broadcasting.

I spoke to the friend in Europe asking if we could buy a second lot of studio equipment through him at trade price. He offered to donate the equipment, but had no way to send it to us. A few days later I was asked to film a conference in Spain. You cannot fly from Cyprus to Spain directly so I flew through the country where the equipment was, that we needed to bring to Cyprus. By the time I arrived at the airport I had about 50kg of excess baggage. You can imagine the reaction of the check-in girl, 'I'm sorry sir, but you have more than two and half times your baggage allowance, I will have to charge you'. I responded that I worked with a British registered charity and that anything she could do would be appreciated. She went away and made a phone call and came back saying that the company said I could take it all for nothing.

Because we don't speak Arabic and we are working with other people who speak the languages, we are doing primarily technical work, production and guidance on content. The

Everyone wants to speak, but nobody wants to listen. They don't think that you have a right to express yourself also. We need to find ways of expressing things clearly and short. If I am given the alternative of writing a novel or a paragraph I will choose the paragraph. Long writing is just wasting words. A lot of words. I feel 'Just give me your summary at the end'. MAX

I love to write – I wrote in Islam and I wrote a lot, I read in order to write. Whatever happens I will carry on writing. Why do I want to write about God? We don't have many Christian books... one day I was talking to some people, 'Islam has lots of books but nobody have their own books... [in their home in the Arabic world]' We don't have enough books talking about our faith in the Messiah and most of those we have are translated from other languages, especially English. It is very sad that we have almost no books about Christianity.

When I read books translated from another language I feel separated from it. I felt that Jesus is not for Arabs, we don't have an Arabic Jesus. The books about Jesus in Arabic are simple, with no depth. They don't study or show depth. In English there are many books, but not in Arabic. I want to make a bridge between the Arabic tongue and a depth of information about Jesus. There are 300 million Arabic speakers and they have nothing to know other than Islam. This is unfair. MAX

actual content is written, recorded etc by others. So we cannot evaluate fully what it is like. We partly evaluate through the popularity or otherwise of the material we produce, and the response to the material. Those are both encouraging.

We have also recently had ours and other people's material evaluated content-wise on a system that we developed, to score how different materials hit their target audience. That too was encouraging.

So if all that's encouraging when I tell people about what we are doing, why do I hate it? There are two reasons. One is that I feel I am telling only half the story. Yes, I do tell about some of our struggles, but not the long term emotional struggles. Secondly, because I generally don't like listening to talks, and so keep thinking of the people in the audience like me who are sitting there wishing they didn't have to listen!

Quite a bit of the time I feel that I am creatively stunted in what we are doing and in what I see others doing. Because I feel that we are not really being as creative as we should be I feel that I am not telling the whole story. Some of what we do is creative, but much is not. A lot is boring.

And that overlaps with the talks that I give to people about what we do. Often I fall asleep in sermons because they are pretty boring. When the vicar from one of the churches in the UK we come from came out to Cyprus a while back, he came to church with me and over lunch admitted to the family he wasn't sure if he should wake me in the sermon as I was sleeping so peacefully.

However, falling asleep in church is not a new phenomenon. In the USA back in Puritan New England they had a 'Tithingman' who would wake up sleeping congregants by poking them with a heavily knobbed staff.[1] Making the sermon or talk the central part of a Christian service was introduced by Luther when he re-formed the Catholic Mass. '*A Christian congregation should never gather together without the preaching of God's word and prayer, no matter how briefly*'[2] and '*the preaching and teaching of God's Word is the most important part of Divine service.*'[3] The pressure towards what we call preaching has more to do with Luther's intellectualising of Christianity than

1 Pagan Christianity by Frank Viola p. 49 where he is referencing Searching Together ,Vol. 11, No. 4 1982 pp 38-39

2 Concerning the Order of Public Worship, Luther's Works, LIII, 11 quoted by Frank Viola in Pagan Christianity p43

3 The German Mass, Luther's Works, LIII, 68 quoted by Frank Viola in Pagan Christianity p43

the practice of the early church.

In my travels and meeting with people from other churches and 'missionaries' I find that my experience of nodding off or latent boredom in a sermon is not unique. I met young post-modern people from one missionary training course. You would expect in that audience they were keen to learn more about the Lord. A small sample, but those who are creative thinkers, admitted the talks 'boring' and 'very basic'.

They tried to find places they could hide during these talks. The leadership spent their time trying to stop them finding places to hide. The reason for trying to hide was that attendance at these sessions had been made mandatory. Similarly when I visited a Christian University in the USA some years ago I discovered that each student had been issued with a swipe-card which they had to swipe when they went into 'devotions' each morning, to prove they had attended.

I think the problem had been addressed the wrong way. Rather than making sessions mandatory, questions should have been asked as to why the sessions were so boring that young people who had dedicated two years of their life [sometimes longer] to serving the Lord found them so boring they wanted to miss them.

If I am presented with a table with only one dish on it, I have no choice, but with many dishes I can chose and there is a richness to it. It is not boring. MAX

In fact in many church situations there is a group, a significant sized group, that are getting more and more bored. They are people for whom didactic teaching holds little or no appeal and who need to engage with the content in dialogue.

Although the post-modern generation has a greater orientation towards service, they also have a greater orientation towards artistic expression and dialogue. Thus our modernist approach to how we do 'teaching' and how we do 'church' is unlikely to touch at a deep level a post-modern generation, whether those people are from the East or from the West.

Most Christian talks, most radio programmes, most TV programmes seem to be 'the Bible says this...' It's what people call expository preaching and many Evangelicals believe it is the way all sermons should be 'preached'. Please don't hear me saying the Bible doesn't matter, I am not saying that at all. The Bible is a record of the Word of God and His dealing with mankind. We are commended in the Bible to test any other revelations against what is in the Bible. The Bereans checked out what Paul was saying to check that what he said was in accordance with what had been revealed before. I believe we should do this a lot more, as we would then realise how many of the modern movements are not in alignment with earlier revelations of God.

Telling stories

As we have already seen, when Jesus was on earth much of the time he didn't do talks along the lines of 'the Bible says this...'. He told stories, interesting stories, creative stories. Sometimes he took existing stories and added creative new ends to them. Paul, when talking to the Athenians[1], used the statue to the unknown god as a hook to introduce his listeners to the God who could be known.

I heard somewhere that the parable of the lost son was in fact a story that was similar to a story circulating in Palestine in Jesus' time, where the young man squandered his inheritance and when he returned the father accepted him back as a hired hand. If this were so it would fit with Jesus creatively taking a story that was well-known and changing the end, giving it a twist we would say now, and giving it new meaning. This would certainly fit with Jesus' radical attitudes elsewhere, turning things upon their head. As a story the listeners would have known, they would have heard and expected one ending but the new ending would have been revolutionary, counter cultural and had them talking among themselves for days.

There is a Bible school I heard about in Africa where the entire curriculum consists of the students learning the stories of the Bible by heart, as stories. These students will work as pastors and church planters in communities that are primarily oral cultures. For villages and towns that communicate by telling stories, learning modern exegetal techniques would be a waste of time.

Within the context of the Middle East, book learning is less important than oral learning. Few people have many books in their homes, and TV dramas which portray stories appear more popular than documentaries. In fact, I have rarely seen an Arabic documentary in the Middle East. It is for that reason that we need to focus on storytelling rather than rationalism and argument to share Christ with the people of the Middle East.

Stories are a very important and effective way to communicate. Everyone in the Arab world loves a story. They don't like statements, they like a story and are attracted by it. Arabic culture is full of stories. In Qu'ran there are a lot of stories which have a large effect on the people.

Stories give them a different way of thinking and it's an acceptable way to communicate an alternative way of thinking. I am writing some stories now and my hope is that people will read them and they will think, 'Yes, these are good ideas' and this will open a door to thinking differently. MAX

Ted Dekker is one Christian author who is doing that these days in English, his alternate realities and unconventional stories clearly contain truth about God, without being direct analogies. He isn't really considered a "Christian" author by many. C.S. Lewis, J.R.R Tolkien, G.K Chesterton, J.K. Rowling are also great Jesus-following story tellers who's books help us to think differently. I believe John Grisham's secular 'The Street Lawyer' should be required reading for all western believers. DAN

---

1 Acts 17:16-34

Paul's talks

There are only two records of talks given by Paul in the Bible. One tells us of the model he used in the Synagogues among the Jews[1] and one tells us of the talk in Athens[2]. Though the content would be different, this second talk mirrors the type of communication we might attempt when telling people from the Middle East about the Messiah. The Athenian talk was the one that could be considered cross-cultural, communicating the message of Jesus to people who knew little of the context into which the Messiah had come.

Paul arrives in Athens and is horrified to see the city full of idols. As a Jew and a Pharisee this would have been an abomination to him. He started by reasoning and arguing with anyone who would listen to him about Jesus and the resurrection. He was apparently getting nowhere, some calling him just a babbler and others perceiving him to be introducing foreign ideas about gods. So they take him to the Areopagus, the central debating hall in Athens. There he addresses the meeting.

He starts off by commending the people of Athens for being religious and uses the example of the very idols that so upset him when he arrived. He then uses one of these, the altar to an 'unknown god' as the starting point for telling them about the living God. Note how he started where they were, and found something to build upon where there was agreement. The Athenians thought of themselves as religious, and so he starts there.

When he starts to talk about God he puts their idols into context. The God who made the world and everything in it doesn't live in temples made by man nor does He need what we make or do. God is in charge of the world and His desire is that we should seek Him, this 'unknown god'.

Paul goes on to say that because He created us we shouldn't think of Him in terms of inanimate objects. In the past this might have been acceptable but now we must change direction because there is a day in the future when He will judge us. The Bible doesn't say that Jesus is the Judge by name, but implies this. Paul says that the proof this man [Jesus] is the Judge is that He was raised from the dead by God.

The reaction to this talk was that some people thought someone coming back from the dead was impossible and so

Paul was a wonderful communicator. He tried to make it easy, to make it clear, not strange for them. I feel it is selfish to have your special [Christian] things, using special words. It is simple and we should use simple words that everyone can understand.

Like Paul we should find ways to communicate with the people. Paul is a good teacher for us to follow in his communication. MAX

1 Acts 17:1-9
2 Acts 17:16-34

sneered at him, others had their interest piqued and wanted to know more, while others became believers.

The things to notice here are almost not what Paul says, but what he doesn't say. Paul doesn't quote the Bible [Old Testament] at all; He doesn't use ideas that would be alien to his audience, like fulfilment of prophecies. He doesn't use any of Jesus' teaching or refer to His miracles. He doesn't encourage people to join his special group, or some kind of separation in any way. He doesn't give any sets of rules on how to live or encourage adherence to any religious pattern of behaviour.

He uses a starting point that is an anathema to him as a strict Pharisee, but which nevertheless is a building block towards his audience understanding his message. He talks about God in general terms, but goes on to challenge people to change and turn to the living God. That turnaround is given in the context of what is an affront to God there, not in theoretical or general terms. His aim is simply to encourage people to have a relationship with the God who is alive and not made of gold, silver or stone.

Stories in the Old Testament

The Old Testament isn't full of stories that communicate a message in the same way as Jesus' parables. In the Old Testament God communicated more through prophets, who proclaimed God's message. One of these prophets, Hosea, was instructed to communicate what God was saying through a real life parable.

When God started to communicate through Hosea, he was told first of all to go and marry a prostitute[1]. The reason for this was to show in story form what God was feeling like towards Israel, that His people were guilty of the worst sins and that He was married to them. So Hosea married Gomer.

When children were born each was named after a particular issue that the Lord had with his people. Hosea's first son was called Jezreel[2] after the sin committed by Jehu in the massacre at Jezreel.

His first daughter was called Ruhamah, a name which sounds like the Hebrew for 'not loved', again to show God's displeasure with the tribe of Israel. His second son was called 'Lo-Ammi' which means 'not my people' and the Lord disavows

The Bible is easier to understand than Christian people [in general], Paul is easier than the Old Testament and Jesus is easier than Paul. But even some of the parables the disciples couldn't understand. So how are Muslims to understand Christian people? MAX

1 Hosea 1:1-11
2 Hosea 1:4

the people of Israel.

The Lord commands Hosea to separate and then reunite with his wife, the prostitute. This involved buying her back out of slavery.

Graphically the Lord uses a story to communicate truth. I cannot imagine what it was like for Hosea, or for a daughter to grow up with a name 'not loved'. Yet this shows that the Lord used creativity in communicating his message.

Another prophet who used a story was Nathan, in his dealing with King David[1]. Kings were dangerous and King David had just had one of his men killed because he wanted Bathsheba for his wife. Instead of directly confronting David, Nathan tells a story.

The story Nathan tells is of two men, one rich, one poor. The rich man had many sheep, but the poor man just one ewe. That ewe was precious to him, eating food with him, drinking with him and slept in his arms. The ewe was like a daughter to him.

When a traveller came to visit the rich man, rather than using one of his own sheep for the feast, he took the ewe that belonged to the poor man. The Bible records that David was angry with what the rich man had done and it was in that context that Nathan confronted David about what he had done with Bathsheba. David's reaction is one of penitence. The story had hit home to him and he was full of remorse.

Communication that keeps people's interest

So why is so much of our communication boring as Christians? We justify what we do by counting the effects... so many people heard, so many people responded. Yes, that is important. But I have the increasing nagging feeling that we are missing out on our calling to be creative, to seek interesting ways to tell people about Jesus and to do it in a style that is first-rate.

For instance, a Middle Eastern friend wrote a story about a mug as a parable of his life. What he wanted to illustrate was how he had felt just one of a crowd, following an identical pattern as everyone else until he discovered Jesus. Jesus, he found, was able to give him choice. He could choose to follow or choose not to follow. This may seem obvious to us, who have

1 2 Samuel 12:1-6

grown up in a culture with a high degree of individualism, but for him this was a significant understanding. Using this story he then went on to illustrate how God offers life in all its fullness, which is better than just being part of a crowd.

To us this story might seem trite or alien, but I watched him tell it to another person from the Middle East. I could see on their face that they loved the style associated with the story. Afterwards, the listener thanked me for introducing him to the storyteller.

Nooma is a series of short films that explore our world from a perspective of Jesus. The producers put it this way[1]:

> *Jesus lived with the awareness that God is doing something, right here, right now, and anybody can be a part of it. He encouraged his listeners to search, to question, to wrestle with the implications of what he was saying and doing. He inspired, challenged, provoked, comforted, and invited people to be open to God's work in this world. Wherever he went, whatever he did, Jesus started discussions about what matters most, because for Jesus, God is always inviting us to open our eyes and join in.*

I felt that there was something behind the words in Nooma. Rob Bell picked subjects that are important and made it easier for people to understand. His language wasn't difficult. He tried to explain the meaning of the Bible. Often when I hear Christians I feel I need to get out the dictionary and try to understand the words. His whole purpose was to explain by examples, by parables, and so he was not hard to understand. MAX

Some of the Nooma DVDs capture this same story telling style. And certainly there are some people who do make us think in the way they communicate. I'm sitting in Hong Kong right now and around me are hundreds of sky scrapers. People here are born, live, work and die in sky scrapers. It's like the computer game Sim-Tower in reality. I have begun to see how the authors of the game got their ideas.

We need to think creatively in the situation we find ourselves. For instance, when I was thinking of Hong Kong a story came to mind that could be used to communicate the gospel but leave people thinking.

I thought of a story of a man in one of the flats who never dealt with his rubbish. Rather than disposing of it correctly he just left it around and this affected the whole skyscraper bringing him into conflict with the manager of the block. The manager would suggest all kinds of solutions to try to reduce the vermin infestation that was affecting everyone. The man would try some for a while, but being lazy would soon fail in some way. Relationship between the manager and the tenant inevitably broke down, and unless there was a way to solve

1 http://nooma.com/

the problem of the rubbish the man would have to be evicted. This was the last thing that the manager wanted.

The manager decided the only answer was to have his son do the cleaning up on the man's behalf. In doing so the managers son fell from the twelfth storey and died. It was only at the funeral that the tenant realised how much the manager cared for him.

It's an obvious story perhaps, but would put the Good News about Jesus into terms that matched the urban life of people in Hong Kong which is very different from the rural lifestyle of Jesus' day. The message is still the same, the vehicle different.

A couple of days ago on a loudspeaker I heard someone sharing their testimony. It went something like this: 'I was born to Christian parents, but as a teenager I rebelled and went away from God. I enjoyed girls and alcohol and my life went downhill. At the bottom I met with God and was saved and became a Christian. Now everything is great.' My two sons reckon almost every speaker at the youth group in Cyprus from one particular church background have the same testimony, and that most of the youth group switch off by the first or second sentence. They have heard it all before.

I think, sadly, the same is true for people from the Middle East hearing the Gospel. They have heard it all before. We believe they have not heard because they have not responded. And it's true that they may not have heard the Gospel in a way that makes sense to them, but most have some [frequently totally untrue] perception of Christianity. What they heard and how they heard it can either be a sermon from a sheik in a mosque [likely to be untrue and inaccurate] or a satellite TV station [which could either appear alien or reinforce their perceptions for the mosque] or they could believe a circulated myth that the west is Christian and the west is into free sex and sin and so Christianity means free sex and sin.

One of the things about the way Jesus communicated the Good News He came to bring, was that it made us think. Frequently He ended what He had to say with something along the lines of 'If you've got open ears to hear, then you'll get this message'. Frequently too His followers said, 'We don't understand, please explain'. Most times I listen to talks from Christians the message is so obvious nobody would ask us to explain. Very infrequently do we have to think about what the person is saying.

If you go as a group to the cinema or theatre it's not

Parables are not there to give you information. They are to be enjoyable to listen to but they are to take you step by step along a road and will almost lead you by the hand. They are like an alphabet. You cannot speak English with just the letters, but with the alphabet you can create words and the words will have meaning. So it is with parables.

When you read a story and hear a parable I cannot expect you to say instantly 'OK, I will change now...' but with parables I am taking you step by step along the way. This is like Jesus, He was taking us step by step. Parables can work with people who are even anti-Christian. MAX

uncommon to meet afterwards and discuss the film or performance; not just the quality of the performance but what the author, director or actors were trying to communicate. It is often irritating after a Christian drama when someone gets up and explains what it means. If the drama didn't make us think then it had failed and shouldn't be done at all. If it made us think then let us think and don't tell us your thoughts.

Preaching and teaching

This brings me on to a difference between preaching and teaching - preaching is proclaiming the Good News of Jesus and teaching refers to teaching followers of Jesus about following Him. From my reading of the Bible, we should proclaim the Gospel to those who are not yet followers and teach those who are. Of course, that brings back the question about how to determine whether someone is a follower or not. That is a significant question with respect to media and one we are looking at in this book. Use a proclaiming/preaching item at people who are already followers and the reaction [internally even if not expressed] is 'I know that already, that's why I decided to follow Jesus'. Of course sometimes it's good to be reminded of the Good News but frequent repetition of a message dulls its effects on the hearer.

Teaching on the other hand is somewhat different. We should note that Jesus' commission to us was to make 'disciples' of people from every nation. *Disciple* comes from the Latin word which means *student* or *learner*. So He was focusing on the learning process rather than the teaching process. Because elsewhere Paul notes 'teacher' as being a spiritual role, there has sometimes been a greater emphasis on the teaching rather than the learning. This has partly arisen as schooling has become more common worldwide and so the expectation upon the teaching/learning has been similar to a school scenario. However, Jesus' method of teaching or training His disciples was closer to an apprenticeship model than a school model. He showed them how to do it, explained how to do it, then got them to do it and then honed their abilities as they worked together and the disciples grew in ability.

Look at, for instance, His reactions to the disciples in the feeding of the 5,000[1], his sending them out in pairs[2] and his reaction to the disciples when they tried to kick a demon

In courses like Iktishaf [Discovery] it's clear and at the end of you can say 'Yes, I will follow Jesus'. But to start something like this you have to be already a long way on the road, after parables that have taken you that far.

When I saw you using diagrams and pictures to struggle with ideas it makes it clear. Like the diagram to show the logic on the parable of the Wedding Feast. I have seen nobody else do that. I wish more people would do it. MAX

1 John 6:1-14
2 Mark 6:5-13

out of someone and failed[1]. All this follows his integration of showing them, explaining and then getting them to 'do the stuff'.

This ought to influence our approaches to media for training followers of Jesus. Most of our training is through people standing at the front of meetings giving talks, the traditional sermon, and the traditional school model. If you look at Jesus' life, the majority of the big meetings were proclaiming the kingdom and the majority of the teaching took place in small meetings. I think this should affect how we do church: The current trend towards the mega-church and towards a highly programmatic method of teaching I believe to be contrary to the method that Jesus used. I also believe it to be broadly speaking ineffective in helping people to live their lives for Jesus.

Different learning styles

Earlier I admitted I fell asleep in most sermons because they are boring. Actually, you should see that statement through post-modern eyes... *for me* they are boring. I don't learn through listening to a talk. I don't think I ever have really. I remember for the last year or two of my life at school spending time so bored and needing to stay awake that I would watch and count the second hand going round on the clock. I then thought if I could survive those 60 seconds I would survive the next 60 seconds and would count them off and so on and so on. In churches, clocks are often at the back for the speaker to see so I cannot use that technique while listening to a sermon!

Other people find other methods of communication helpful. We recently attended a 'Walk thru the New Testament' programme. I think it was misnamed and should have been 'Dance through the New Testament', since the programme focussed on leaning kinaesthetically what appeared to me to be something similar to a hand jive. Don't get me wrong, I thought it was great... *for some people*. For me, within about 10 minutes, I was hopelessly lost and following everyone else about one or two steps behind. Much like the way I dance I guess! For me, I wished they had a topographical map of the area so I could study it and see in my mind's eye the walk through the New Testament.

Other people find books the easiest way to gather

1 Mark 9:14-32

information. I admit I love books too, and for some things reading a book is the easiest way for me to learn. Certainly I think I learn from books about 100 times more easily than I do from listening to a talk. I hear the voice of the author or the characters in a book as I am reading, which would indicate that I am an aural learner to some degree, so I am not sure why I prefer books to talks.

Primarily I think I find I learn best from visuals, I have just been reading a book by Frank Viola titled 'Pagan Christianity' where he outlines the various pagan influences that have shaped the church of today. Though the book was fascinating in its detail, I would have liked diagrams to show the influences and how they came into the church. That would have helped me a lot.

So, when we are thinking about communicating the Gospel we must always remember people are different. Each person is unique. Whereas Jesus employed parables or stories to communicate with the crowds who followed him, some people will be left cold by this and say 'give me the facts, stop talking around the subject'.

How you learn or listen is partly innate, something God created in you and partly conditioned by the culture or family you grew up in. Children who grow up in families with many books and parents that love books are more likely to enjoy reading and take in information through books.

Creativity

Last weekend a friend of mine died. Elias was a highly creative person. He painted extremely well, sang and wrote songs to God. The songs I could not understand as they were in Greek, but they sounded very good when he sang them and when he translated them for me the thoughts were expressing his and our adoration of our Lord.

Elias encouraged me to paint, too. I went to his art classes for a year. It was a fascinating experience learning to paint and draw and at the same time get to know Elias better. My grandmother painted and I used to love watching her paintings develop. Many were left around the place as she was a terribly untidy person. She lived at the opposite end of the country and by the time she came to live in our town she was sadly too old and frail to paint any more.

Elias taught me about negative space and about textures and colours, but the thing that I learnt most in my art classes was about seeing. We look but do not see in everyday life. I know that sounds like something Jesus said - 'they look but do not see, hear but do not understand'[1] - and there are parallels. But in this case I particularly mean about colour.

As an example we think of the flesh colour of a western European as being pink - that is how we would describe it as a child and colouring in a drawing as a child we might use a pink crayon. But looking, really looking, we see many subtle tints and shades and tones. We might need to use blue or magenta or greens to create the right feeling for a face. But a casual glance at a face would just see the face as pink.

I found at Elias' art classes that if I was stressed I could not draw or paint. The reason was that I could not see to be able to draw or paint. Those shades of colour, shades of light and dark were almost impossible to see.

The final thing I found was that because drawing or painting was an introverted activity, something coming out from inside of you, I could only do this if I had enough extroverted time during the week. If I had spent the week working alone and with very few meetings with other people I would want to spend the time chatting with Elias. Yes, I would draw and paint, but it was nothing really other than being in the same room and interacting with him. The drawing was dead and lifeless.

1 Luke 8:10

Whenever I write, I don't want to be the most important writer, I don't want to be the best writer in the world. No, I want to make the writing itself as much as possible perfect. I mean that I chose the words with great care – I use all my experience. I want to be generous. I will give everything into even one paragraph. I walk round on my balcony reading aloud so I can choose each and every word with care.

My purpose is not to please the audience. I might tear something up and friends might say 'Why are you doing this, it is good?' But I want to be perfect with my creation. As perfect as I can be in the writing. MAX

The creativity for me only came when I had interacted with others during the week. Others I am sure are different. I think it depends whether you are an introvert or extrovert – for the introvert the internal activity recharges them, for the extrovert they recharge with others and only have the energy for internal activity if they are already recharged!

I think it's very important that we develop our creative nature and produce media that is both interesting and to a high quality. After all, when God created the earth He said it was good, and we are created in the image of God with the same inbuilt nature to be creative.

One of the major inhibitors of creativity is a lack of resources. Today I saw some of the most battered, damaged microphones I have seen anywhere in the world. They belong to a group that performs all over the world. The reason they are so battered is not because they have been heavily used, but because they are carried around in a thin canvas bag with cables and other audio pieces thrown on top. Alongside these were microphone stands which had lost their adjusting knobs and were held together with string.

Internally I am screaming. This is not a group overflowing with money. They, like us, are very short of resources. I want to scream out loud, but it would not do any good. The trouble is I don't know if God is screaming with me or against me. Does he see this as an act of poor stewardship or my attitude as unnecessary concern. Or both. A paradox?

This is not an isolated example. Within the last year or so I have seen two video cameras in one country destroyed due to carelessness. In another country I was shown a brand new laptop computer with a cracked screen – destroyed because the worker didn't want to carry it as 'carry on' baggage and sent it as checked baggage in his suitcase.

Each time internally I scream. We in missions have little resources, but frequently I see those resources ill used and not cared for. And it's not just financial resources we lack, it's also manpower that limits us. We are providing Internet resources and facilities for a number of other organizations. Because we are doing this we don't have the time to develop the more creative projects we feel called to. Simple answer: Drop providing resources and do the creative projects. This is not possible as we need those Internet resources and facilities to do those creative projects. We need more staff. We talk to other groups. All are short of people. Again internally I scream. Is God screaming with me or against me?

Time seems another problem. Recently I was hearing about a project that is years late and taking every penny this group has to try to complete, to the detriment of other existing projects. Primarily this was caused by poor management.

Two of the projects we have been involved with were 9-12 months late. In both cases this was because the equipment we had was old and unreliable, the computer video editing system crashed and crashed, and the software didn't behave as it should. We replaced the video editing equipment half way through the second project, but that was also delayed due to people elsewhere in the chain doing a very bad job and this took us vast numbers of hours to correct. Internally I was screaming.

Creativity is costly for the creator, partly because the very act of creating takes something of the creator. But in the missions world there seems to be extra layers of pain. We often spiritualise this, putting it down to attacks of the devil. Certainly we have attacks from Satan, and he attacks through equipment failure, people and management. But increasingly I am feeling that he is maybe getting credit for some things that are just plain bad stewardship.

In the Christian world there is a push towards greater accountability. There is one area which I believe a high level of accountability is non-negotiable. Handling money is that area. However, what I have observed happening is over-managing in the name of accountability. Frequently we get more and more management, with more and more documentation which takes time away from anything creative. The Bible is clear about a man counting the cost of building before starting[1]. Yet paradoxically if we accurately counted the cost before we started, much of what we do in missions wouldn't get done. There is a step of faith involved as well as accountability.

Secondly accountability implies measuring, counting something. The measuring and counting is very much counter to creativity and to post-modern thought. I find myself pulled in two directions at the same time over this - I am enough of a child of modernism to want to somehow count and measure and evaluate what we do, and a child of post-modernism that hates doing so. This may be why it has taken so long to find ways of evaluating what we are doing, and why the result is more narrative orientated than statistically. Creativity looks more towards narrative than numbers.

1 Luke 14:28-30

In the image...

Where it all started was in what we call the Garden of Eden. At the centre of the garden there were two trees: the tree of the knowledge of good and evil and the tree of everlasting life. God said 'Don't eat from the tree of the knowledge of good and evil'. He said nothing about the tree of everlasting life.

When the first man and woman ate from the tree of the knowledge of good and evil God was upset with them for disobedience[1]. He said that they had now become 'like one of us, knowing good and evil' and kicked them out of the garden so that they wouldn't eat from the tree of eternal life and also become like God living for eternity.

Why did God *not* want us to know the difference between good and evil? Why was He happy for mankind to live forever if they didn't know good and evil, and not when they did? If mankind didn't know the difference between good and evil what kind of relationship would have been between God and mankind? Would God have become bored with that relationship?

What I am really thinking is that there is a paradox here. Without the knowledge of good and evil there is no real free will, because without that knowledge you cannot know to chose. Now God created man with free will, but without the knowledge of good and evil. So, if Adam and Eve didn't have the knowledge of good and evil how did they know not to eat the fruit of the tree of the knowledge of good and evil. Answer because God told them... but... before they ate it they didn't have the knowledge that it was wrong. So it was inevitable they would eat it.

What was God looking for in the relationship with Adam and Eve if they didn't know what was good and what was evil?

I am coming to believe that a true understanding of God is about paradox and symmetry and that is what separates followers of the one true God from all others. That we don't need a neat packaged system with all the bugs worked out - we follow a living God with all the paradoxes there are in Him.

If that perception is true, then that could explain why I am seeing so many problems with some parts of the church

1 Genesis 3

God is the most important creator and He teaches us how to be creative people. I love nature and I love His creation and in my writing I am trying to be creative too. MAX

and with the way we communicate the truth of the Gospel. Modernist Evangelicalism wants to worship a God with all the bugs worked out. They are thus demeaning Him to the level of other gods, and in reality not worshipping the one true God. '*In religion, it is not the sycophants or those who cling most faithfully to the status quo who are ultimately praised*'[1]:

> *Perhaps we need a churchless Church.*
>
> *The body of Christ is a given - we have to belong to the Church [macro]. But perhaps we should give up calling the things we are involved in church [micro]. It is just such an unhelpful and loaded word to use. "Do you want to come to church?" To be honest, no I don't. And by the numbers and temper of those in the debate, there's plenty of others who don't either. Church can be something I am a part of. But it's not something I want to 'go to'.* [2]

Is the problem with going to church really that it packages things up too neatly and creates a paradox-free sycophantic religion that Jesus came to abolish? Back to Rollo May again:

> *Those we call saints rebelled against an outmoded and inadequate form of God on the basis of their new insights into divinity... Their rebellion was motivated by new insights into the meaning of godliness. They rebelled, as Paul Tillich has so beautifully stated, against God in the name of the God beyond God. The continuous emergence of the God beyond God is the mark of creative courage in the religious sphere.*[3]

But that is not his central thesis which is:

> *I shall explore the hypothesis that limits are not only unavoidable in human life, they are also valuable. I shall discuss the phenomenon that creativity itself requires limits, for the creative act arises out of the struggle of human beings with and against that which limits them.*[4]

Christians have a very large treasure but most people don't use it. I feel like I am seeing a rich person who can use his money in a wonderful way but he lives in a poor way. He leaves his money in the bank and lives a poor life. Christians don't use the breadth of what is available. They don't want to struggle with their minds. They just repeat again and again without struggling. I feel like shouting 'You can use more of this valuable resource'. MAX

1 P31, The courage to create, Rollo May
2 The Complex Christ, blog by Kester Bewin
3 P32,The courage to create, Rollo May
4 P134,The courage to create, Rollo May

Citing the start of human consciousness in the Garden of Eden as a portrayal in the context of a rebellion, struggling against a limit, Rollo goes on to say how, punished by God, Adam and Eve get other limits - anxiety, the feeling of alienation and guilt. But, he claims, valuable qualities come out of this: *sense of personal responsibility and ultimately the possibility, born out of loneliness, of human love.* But he concludes, *Confronting limits for the human personality actually turns out to be expansive. Limiting and expanding thus go together.*[1]

Using the example of a river and river bank, Rollo believes that in creativity *limits are as necessary as those provided by the banks of a river, without which the water would be dispersed on the earth and there would be no river - that is, the river is constituted by the tension between the flowing water and the banks. Art in the same way requires limits as a necessary factor in it's birth. Creativity arises out of a tension between spontaneity and limitations.*[2]

Thinking of the limitation of the canvas upon the painter as a boundary to their work I was reminded of a work by Martin Honert entitled Kinderkreussug which he developed between 1995 and 1997. In this work of art Honert does not allow himself to be limited by the canvas but marching out from the acrylic are three dimensional characters, confronting the viewer with the edge between flat art and sculpture.

Honert claimed to be motivated in his art by *...the emotional confusion of pathos and embarrassment, seriousness and absurdity, demand and reality, the sad ending of a happy time*[3]. He looks on in seeing not so much a struggling against the boundaries or limits but in seeing the paradox or symmetry of life.

Personally, I think in fact the struggle with limits as Rollo May puts it is not really a struggle with limits but a struggle with rationalism to reconcile these paradoxes we call human life. Is it the river that defines the river bank or the bank that defines the river? Though the eastern way of looking at life doesn't contain all truth, the easterner sees and expresses this balance as 'yin and yan'. Those of us who assert that there is a God and that He loves us are confronted with another group of humans who assert that there is no God, or that if there is He is severe and that we cannot know Him.

1 P136-137,The courage to create, Rollo May
2 P137,The courage to create, Rollo May
3 P242/243,Art at the Turn of the Millennium

Nobody expresses this better for me than Tom Stoppard, in his play ***Jumpers***, which claims to be *a serious attempt to debate the existence of a moral absolute, of metaphysical reality, of God...* Stoppard provides George, the main perpetrator of this debate, with this closing monologue:

> *'A remarkable number of apparently intelligent people are baffled by the fact a different group of apparently intelligent people profess to a knowledge of God when common sense tells them - the first group of apparently intelligent people - that knowledge is only a possibility in matters which can be demonstrated to be true or false, as that the Bristol train leaves from Paddington. And yet these same apparently intelligent people, who in extreme cases will not even admit that the Bristol train left from Paddington yesterday - which might be a malicious report or a collective trick of memory - nor that it will leave from there tomorrow - for nothing is certain - and will only agree that it did today if they were actually there when it left - and even then only on the understanding that all the observable phenomena associated with the train leaving Paddington could equally well be accounted for by Paddington leaving the train - these same people will, nevertheless, and without any sense of inconsistency, claim to know that life is better than death, that love is better than hate, and that the light shining through the east window of the bloody gymnasium is more beautiful than a rotting corpse!'*[1]

Art and creativity is not merely about beauty but is about expressing this tension, and in the last few decades we have seen the limits pushed further and further. For example Henrik Plenge Jacobson in collaboration with Jes Brinch created a rotting corpse entitled ***Teacher*** for the 'Human Conditions' exhibition in 1997 in Finland[2].

This is not a sculpture I think I would ever create, and it begs the question that Rollo May asks earlier in his book: *The fact that talent is plentiful but passion is lacking seems to me to be a fundamental facet of the problem of creativity in*

1 Jumpers, Tom Stoppard
2 P264-265, Art at the Turn of the Millennium

many fields today, and our ways of approaching creativity by avoiding the encounter have played directly into this trend. We worship technique - talent - as a way of evading the anxiety of the direct encounter.[1]

The limits to what is and isn't art and what is creativity in art are further confused when we look at someone like Vanessa Beechcroft's works. In her exhibition openings and performances she has a group of girls silently take up positions, moving very little, standing before their public like living pictures. This is like looking at a mirror in some ways, seeing ourselves; well, not ourselves, but humankind. Vanessa says '*I am interested in the difference between what I expect and what actually happens*'[2].

Actually I believe there is always something unexpected in the creative process. I wonder whether it was somewhat unexpected for God when he created the world. Thinking about Rollo May's assertion that creativity is about limits and expansion, I wonder how that relates to the primary act of creation by God.

We think of His creation in terms of the earth, the universe, mankind, etc. However, we know that there is no end to the universe and in fact many secular scholars now talk about how it is actually rather unexpected that the universe is continually expanding. The creativity is a process without end. It certainly did not, does not and will not have limits or boundaries; it is quite literally expanding.

Is the message clear? I doubt if the message of the piece is anything to do with everything, or wrongness... We could be overly analyzing it, but does the target represent idealism, and the everything is wrong statement say that our idealism is unattainable? DAN

Henrik Jacobson again, '*For me, art should not restrict itself to formal questions. It should represent an alternative, not an assertion. Maybe I'm idealistic, but I think art should be an instrument of criticism.*[3]' Where May talks about limits, here Jacobson also talks about alternative or in some ways paradox or symmetry.

Maybe Jacobson's criticism can be seen in his work ***Everything is wrong***. It's a simple target like an archery target painted in acrylic with the words overlaid. I guess, at least, there is no ambiguity to his message!

It's not a work of beauty, nor a work like his rotting corpse. I find these abstract works to be often more difficult to understand, even though they appear to be clear at first sight.

1 P101,The courage to create, Rollo May
2 P66-67, Art at the Turn of the Millennium
3 P264-265, Art at the Turn of the Millennium

Or is the "Everything is Wrong" statement part of the target, and he is inviting people to shoot down the statement by putting it on a target?

By saying he wants art to be an instrument of criticism, is he saying that by creating artistic works he means to criticize, or that his works should be used as instruments to criticize the world (by others, or himself)? Maybe by setting up statements that let people criticize the world through their reaction to it? Or is his artistic work actually the emotional reaction generated in others to statements such as "Everything is Wrong"? The target is calling out "shoot at me! shoot at me!" and the collected metaphorical bulletholes are his real "work of art"? DAN

So... braving all I decide on a creative act of symmetry for Jacobson's, mine is entitled ***Cake is everything***.

So if everything is wrong and cake is everything... it must prove that cake is wrong!

No?

Oh well...

Art and creativity answer questions in a different way to the way we have been taught by modernism to ask them. They tell a narrative rather than create a logical disputation. They ask and answer questions about life at a deeper level. We have Greek philosophy to thank for separating the spiritual from the earthly. This is modernism. This was never the way God intended and not the way that the Jews understood life. Art also merges the spiritual and the earthly in a way that is closer to pre- and post-modernism.

Lest we get too serious, maybe at this point I should quote two entries by Adrian Plass in his book Bacon Sandwiches and Salvation, which he claims is an A-Z of the Christian Life:

> *Art: something regarded with deep suspicion by many folk in the church. This sad prejudice was exemplified at the Spring Harvest art gallery a few years ago, when someone wrote in the comments book: 'Too many bottoms for my liking.' Particularly frustrating when one reflects that most of the great art produced over the years was influenced by Christian belief.*
>
> *Icon: (1) a devotional painting or carving, usually on wood of Christ or another holy figure (2) it is not generally known that, as a creative race, icon artists are less than confident. When addressing them on the subject of their art, one should look very directly into their faces and express one's response to their work with delicacy and subtlety. This is known in artistic circles as icon-tact.*[1]

The evangelical church has frequently rejected the icons of the Orthodox and the candles of the Catholics. Although I don't personally like the style or the attitude of some Orthodox to icons, I am fairly sure that had I been born 1900 years ago I would have been an icon painter – to attempt to communicate the Gospel using the media of the day. So I feel

1 Bacon Sandwiches and Salvation, Adrian Plass

we cannot reject them out of hand.

Recently art has got a bad name for itself with canvases that are blank or sculptures that are merely a stack of bricks. As we were made in the image of a creative God, we must be careful not to err on the side of accepting any old rubbish as art and not rejecting art because it does not communicate with us from our culture.

This is a pastel drawing I did more than a couple of years ago which is in the entrance to our office. It's there to remind us that though much of what we do is technical, it is the people that matter. It's there to give eye-contact with the audience we never see.

Reading this you may be wondering what I am trying to communicate about creativity and art and how it relates to communicating the Gospel. My conclusion is actually to reject Rollo May's assertion that *Creativity arises out of a tension between spontaneity and limitations.* I believe this is not actually the starting point for creativity but the starting point is paradox and symmetry; and that the tension between spontaneity and limitations is actually an outworking of that paradox and symmetry.

My question arising from this is whether much of the church's monochrome approach to teaching is actually counter to God's creativity in the world. I'm not advocating a pluralistic 'everything goes' approach, but an acceptance of the ambiguity that arises from a relationship with a creative God and an understanding that because we are created in His image there will be ambiguity and paradox in our lives and our worship.

The ultimate act of creativity we are involved with is bringing new human beings into the world and caring for them. That is surely symmetry for God's relationship to us.

This wire-frame sculpture I saw in Singapore - I wish I had noted the name of the sculptor, but there was no name on the work. It expresses that relationship of parent to child. The light air passing through and around the sculpture gives a solid yet almost nonexistent quality to the man and the child. Much like the relationship between God and us as His children where the relationship is apparent and obvious yet experienced without the same solidness of the human relationship that mirrors the original one.

I had been about to say that since we are made in the image of God, I believe our ultimate worship of Him should seek to express that creativity, but realised that could be ambiguous as I believe the ultimate act of God's creativity was in creating humankind. We probably have to be careful or the readings from Song of Songs could change the whole tone of Sunday morning 'worship'.

Story telling is very definitely an art form and, as we have seen, Jesus was one of the key story tellers of all time. He had a sense of both timing and structure.

Many times even Jesus' closest friends asked for an explanation. In our rationalism we want everything so plain that everyone understands everything. Yet this is not what we have seen as the way of God down through the ages. To me it seems in our desire for a mechanistic 'all answers' church we have created something alien to the historical people of God. We have lost creativity and here let me paraphrase Rollo May:

> *The fact that church is plentiful but passion is lacking seems to me to be a fundamental facet of the problem of worship today, and our ways of approaching worship by avoiding the encounter have played directly into this trend. We elevate technique as a way of evading the anxiety of the direct encounter [with God and others].*

I fear we have lost the direct encounter with the living God and replaced it with a synthetic plastic alternative. The debate about church usually surrounds form rather than substance, yet for me form can so easily obfuscate substance. In my experience real direct encounter only takes place within a small group of Jesus-followers. The rest is as insubstantial as the parent and child in the wire frame, not an incarnational living relationship with God.

Having replaced the encounter with a weekly repeatable programmed experience we have totally lost the creativity which was a vital part of encountering (a creative) God.

Charles Finney (1792-1875) could be considered to be the father of modern mass evangelism. Finney spent his time trying to remove creativity.

Finney was a lawyer and brilliant administrator. He sought to organize the 'revivalist' meetings and put so much effort on human endeavour he was [as John Finney put it] 'in danger of denying the grace of God and the work of the Holy Spirit'. Charles Finney is quoted as saying 'A revival is not a miracle, or dependent upon a miracle, in any sense. It's purely

We love to hear stories. We have a history of stories. We accept and love stories. I think that throughout the world stories affect people. In the Qu'ran and the Hadith there are a lot of stories. MAX

Muslims don't look at Christianity as a faith or as a relationship with God. They always see it as a religion. When they see it as a religion they see it as a competition between mosque and church, each vying for more customers! I'm not sure but I think that Christian people in the Middle East think the same way. MAX

philosophical results from the right use of constituted means as much as any other effect produced by the application of means'.

Looking at the history of the church since the first century, it seems to read like a spiral of God doing something creative and new, and man trying to organize it, and in the process crushing all life out of it.

Frank Viola, in a book entitled 'Pagan Christianity', shows how time and time again the church assimilated pagan practices. Frequently these resulted in a legalistic approach. Even Viola, in rejecting all these pagan practices, introduces a legalism and structure that has God unable to do anything in a new way since the time of the apostles!

At the same time, there are new initiatives and the now famous 'barking like dogs' of the Toronto blessing leave us equally bewildered as to whether this is of God or not. Is this a new creative way the Lord is expressing himself?

This question reminds me of a time meeting with a group of young people from the Middle East. These young people were in their twenties and after a very enjoyable meal together they asked me whether I thought it was OK to go to the cinema. The reason for asking they said was that their Christian parents thought it was evil, but they were not so sure.

As well as pointing out the rift in culture between parents and children in the region, this highlighted another issue. These young people had been taught everything in terms of things being black and white, right or wrong. So, confronted with something new, they would not have been equipped to know how to make a decision. I spent the next hour or so talking with them about how we make decisions in the West.

Coming from an evangelical background, I might recite that 'the Bible is the final authority in all matters of faith and conduct' almost as a creedal statement. And I still stand by that as a core belief. However, legalistically extracting sentences or phrases from the Bible and using them as our rules for daily living makes us close to the Pharisees and out of touch with our Lord who frequently broke those laws.

Our understanding of Scripture is not only affected by our geographic culture but also by a temporal culture. I recently enjoyed the film 'Amazing Grace' on one of the long haul flights I was taking. This film tells the story of William Wilberforce, who as a Christian, was instrumental in abolishing the slave trade. Till 1807, few Christians questioned slavery, and used

Maybe the problem with people in general – not just Muslims – is they don't want to open their minds to new ideas, they want to stick with what they are used to. For me in the beginning it was easier not to struggle with new ideas. Even now, a few years into being a follower of the Messiah, there are still many ideas to struggle with. For some people even if you give people all the facts in an easy way then he will not receive it as it is the work of God to draw people to Himself and open their minds. MAX

We have an Arabic proverb: 'We want you to see your future' – means to be husband or wife. You mean nothing in my society unless you are married. This disturbed me – they saw me as only a husband or wife? Everything else is secondary and not important. They cannot accept you as a person. Marriage will not add to me – I am me. Of course I want to marry, but it doesn't make me.

All around the area there are TVs in the restaurants and coffee shops and they show only two things – news and football. And this influence us. MAX

The people who want to know, who want to open their hearts and minds to God. In this area stories play a significant role – they want to see what other people are thinking. I imagine that we separate between what we receive and what is inside us. Many people in the Middle East watched the passion of the Christ, even imams. Everyone was interested to see it. But was it just enjoyment? An hour of pleasure? Many people do want to know and are searching and with them stories can work to draw them to the Lord.

But do stories work by themselves? Yes, of course. If you put good seed in bad soil and nothing happens iot is no good saying the seed is bad because it doesn't bear fruit. No. MAX

passages from Scripture to back up their beliefs.

Whilst maintaining that the Bible is the final authority in all matters of faith and conduct on matters which it speaks, we should not lose contact with the crimson thread that runs through Scripture and tells the bigger picture of God's creative relationship with mankind and of His nature, which helps us to understand the words in the book. His nature is Grace.

Philip Yancey in *What's so amazing about Grace* puts it succinctly:

> *'There is nothing we can do to make God love us more and there is nothing we can do to make God love us less.' He quotes H Richard Neibur, 'The great Christian revolutions come not by the discovery of something that was not known before. They happen when somebody takes radically something that was always there.'*[1]

The revolution we face today is to rediscover and take radically God's creativity in our communication of the Gospel. It will affect our lives, our churches and those he loves who are yet to become followers of the Messiah.

1 What's so amazing about Grace? Philip Yancey pp 13-14

Face to face with the Truth

There are various approaches to sharing Jesus, especially with the people of the Middle East. Some appear mutually opposites: Contrast bridge-building with apologetic denunciation of Islam. Feelings can get petty heated with the denunciators claiming that the bridge-builders are syncretistic and the bridge-builders claiming the denunciators are locked into an Old Testament separatist religion.

These debates can be unhelpful, dividing those people who follow Jesus into separate camps. However, the different camps also perceive the other camps to be at least equally unhelpful, if not downright unsound. In reading a sailing magazine recently I heard about a yacht that was nearly destroyed because the chart was two degrees off. Two degrees is not much. It made me feel that maybe when we are spiritually two degrees off we might be missing the mark as followers of Jesus.

We need to re-look at how we see truth. Brian McLaren put it this way:

> *'I often hear Christians beating the drum of "Absolute truth! Absolute truth!" and I wonder if they know what they're against (relativism, nihilism, hedonism) or in favor of. Are they for this myth of objectivism – an Elightenment ideal that's not a biblical category? Are the for absolute knowledge – the idea that humans are capable (with or without the Bible) of absolute, bulletproof, undoubtable, inerrant knowledge (even the Bible itself says, "we know in part")? Our brethren would do well to ponder these paragraphs and let themselves get rocked and unsettled for a while.'* [1]

I do believe in absolute truth. However, often I think we are unable to see that absolute truth due to the grid through which we see the world. I love a passage in the final book of the CS Lewis' trilogy *That Hideous Strength* where he takes us to a scene of a dialogue between someone from earth and an angelic being. He describes how initially it looks like the heavenly being is floating at an angle to the room, and when you look further you realise that the angel is in fact upright,

1 Post-modern Youth Ministry - Tony Jones - page 201

You have two options - facts and information and serious direct thoughts and alternatively use stories or jokes as examples to communicate. You can use both. When you use one it doesn't mean that you totally disregard the other. But for me, I read factual books and focus on information, but even for me I enjoy a good story to help clarify something.

For people who love to study or think, facts are useful. Most people in the Middle East are not like that - parables or examples are better for them. For some people, even if they are not simple people, if they have closed their minds you cannot do anything using facts and information with them. MAX

In general people are lazy in their minds, they don't want to think or search or investigate. It's enough for the imam to say a word and they will agree with him.

Imams might tell lies about Christianity – that they are not good people and things like that – and people don't want to think and search and verify if it's true.

They look at things to prove that Islam is the truth regardless of the facts. For example, if I debate with you about Christianity, I will become angry and shout and that is enough. Nobody is prepared to say they don't have an answer. I don't look at the facts I just attack you. MAX

being from a greater 'upright' than we perceive on earth. This is similar to the experience of being inside a ship and looking out of a porthole and it appearing we are sailing uphill. Our 'upright' is determined by our surroundings; flat appears flat relative to our location.

I think it's important to realise when we are communicating to Muslims, especially post-modern Muslims, that they and we are both experiencing this sailing uphill effect. The major difference is that we as followers of Jesus are allowed to go out on deck and see where the horizon is. Traditional Islam doesn't allow for questioning. We do and should question. Consider the reaction of Christians to Copernicus when he first suggested the earth was in orbit around the sun. He was considered by Protestants and Catholics alike to be a heretic. What this challenges is our attitude to Scripture.

I was travelling around Larnaka with a friend of mine from Denmark. He is a theatre director of international repute. We had just been out sailing together and had a really great time. Driving back, the topic of conversation turned to God and my faith. My friend is an atheist and post-modern in outlook.

Tony Jones in his book *Post-modern Youth Ministry* starts by explaining his first contact with someone who thought as a post-modern. I expect many of us have had similar experiences:

> *'Upon examining the claims of Christ,' I boldly said, 'we must declare him either the Lord, a liar, or a lunatic.'*
>
> *'Well, I believe he is Lord for you,' came the response.*
>
> *'I must not have explained myself,' I said. 'He claimed not just to be Lord for Tony but for all humanity – in fact for all creation.'*
>
> *'That's fine. I believe that for you, he is Lord of all creation.'*
>
> *'But he claims to be Lord of all creation for everyone.'*
>
> *'Okay, for you he's Lord of all creation for everyone.'*[1]

1 Post-modern Youth Ministry – Tony Jones

Unlike Tony, understanding my friend's post-modern outlook, I decided that if he was ever to come to know Jesus he needed to see that not only is Jesus Lord, but He also wants a personal relationship with him. It's about dialogue. Of course, he would first have to come to accept that Jesus exists, a step prior to Tony's discussion. I tend to assert things in much the same way as Tony, but I hope I am happier to accept the 'for you' of other people, even if I am dealing with something that is ultimate truth.

Sharing a belief that Jesus is Lord amongst Muslim fundamentalists would have the opposite reaction, where they would see a claim that Jesus is Lord to be blasphemy and that we should die. However, the vast majority of people are more tolerant and would see us as either misled or, more commonly among the young people, in an almost identical way to that young person. It is for that reason that I personally believe argument is pointless. Instead building bridges toward people enables real dialogue to take place.

In the West we have developed an attitude towards Biblical truth that many Christians under persecution do not have. A friend of mine used to regularly visit Yemen. In Yemen he met with a follower of Jesus who had been called in by the police many times about his faith. Each time he was tortured. Each time the torture was worse. This Christian under persecution one day asked my friend 'Do you think one day they will kill me?' Reluctantly he replied 'Yes, eventually they will martyr you for your faith'.

Richard Wurmbrand was a Christian pastor at the time of the Russian invasion of Romania in 1948. Wurmbrand was the only one out of four thousand priests and pastors to speak out publicly against the Communists during a national convention of the leading clergy, sponsored by the newly imposed totalitarian government. As a result of his witness he was imprisoned and tortured for fourteen years.

> *Many Christians have asked Wurmbrand. 'Which Scriptures helped you endure your torture?'*
>
> *'Christians,' Wurmbrand wrote, 'were tied to crosses for three days and three nights. The crosses were laid on the floor at different times of the day, and the other*

Whenever I hear a sheik or imam, I ask 'What is he talking about? He isn't checking the truth, he is just filling time. If you want to follow Islam, this is your choice, but please respect yourself and other and base your thinking on logic'. We live in perpetual laziness in our minds. MAX

prisoners were tortured in such as way as to force them to relieve their bodily necessities on the faces of these men. Then the crosses were erected again.'

'One does not 'hang' on a cross,' he said. 'Your body cries out in agony at the torment of the pain, so you twist and turn to find a more comfortable position, only to find that the new one is more painful than the last. You do not hang upon a cross, you writhe in endless agony.'

'In such conditions we knew the verse, 'My grace is sufficient for you.' But the verse 'My grace is sufficient' was not sufficient. We also knew the twenty third psalm, 'The Lord is my Shepherd, I shall not want.' But the psalm about the Shepherd did not help us. A verse about grace was not sufficient; we needed grace. A psalm about the Shepherd was not sufficient; we needed the Shepherd Himself. No verse on earth could enable us to endure such torture.'

'In the West,' Wurmbrand writes, *'I see a danger of Christians worshipping the Bible... The Bible is not 'the Truth', God is 'the Truth.' The Bible is 'the truth about the Truth.' Theology, if it is the right theology, is 'the truth about the truth about the Truth.' And a good sermon is 'the truth about the truth about the truth about the Truth.' And Christian people [in the West] live in these many truths about the Truth, and, because of them, have not 'the Truth.'* [1]

In order to reconcile our angle on truth, we often end up coming together with like-minded people in groups, be those groups churches or mission agencies or other associations. I know I tend to. Followers of Jesus with radically different ideas to mine don't usually challenge me to think, they usually make me feel distanced from them, or question whether they are leading people astray. Although 'radically different' is relative, as followers of Jesus they are going in the same

1 Pp 234-235 'The Children of God' by Deborah (Linda Berg) Davis

direction (I hope) but my feelings are that they are like the yacht that was nearly destroyed because the chart was 2 degrees off.

Philip Yancey expressed exactly my thoughts, feelings and questioning in the start of his book Soul Survivor.

> *I have spent most of my life in recovery from the church. One church I attended during formative years in Georgie of the 1960s presented a hermetically sealed view of the world. A sign out front proudly proclaimed our identity with the words radiating from a many-pointed star: 'New Testament, Blood-bought, Born-again, Premillennial, Dispensational, Fundamental...' Our little group of 200 people had a corner on the truth, God's truth, and everyone who disagreed with us was surely teetering on the edge of hell.*[1]

I was recently challenged to think by a Muslim background believer in these terms: '*Water in one place becomes stagnant and smells bad, but a flowing river refreshes.*' How many of us have recently thought outside the box and got new ideas that are refreshing? That I believe is the creativity that God gave us, which indeed we inherited from Him and yet we are bad at using it. The living water that Jesus offers can itself become stagnant if we are drawing out of the same tank day after day. The manna in the desert was good for one day only, tomorrow's food was only available tomorrow.

What I am trying to do in the stories I am writing is to disturb the reader enough from their non-thinking into questioning so that they might see outside of their closed system long enough to see the truth. I want them to think. I want them to look outside of the box and to search for the truth. I am a peacemaker for those who want to know truth and a troublemaker for those who don't. MAX

1 Soul Survivor – Philip Yancey – page 1

Personal relationship

I had been looking for a way to express God's desire for a relationship with us when I came across this account of Richard Wurmbrand continuing to share his faith during the time he was in prison.

> *One day he was talking with one of the Russian soldiers who had invaded his country – a thinker/intellectual by nature of his rank. Wurmbrand asked him, 'Do you believe in God?'*
>
> *Wurmbrand explained that if he had answered 'No', it would have been understandable since there are many who don't believe in God.*
>
> *However, Wurmbrand recalled, '... he lifted toward me eyes without understanding and gave me an answer which rent my heart in pieces. He said, 'We have no order to believe; if we have an order from Stalin, we will believe.' I had seen for the first time a man who was no more a man. He was a brainwashed tool in the hands of the Communists. He had lost the greatest gift which God has given to a man: To be a personality of his own, who can say yes or no to his fellowman, who can say yes or no, even to God! This Russian soldier could say neither yes nor no. He expected from Stalin his order to believe.'*
>
> *Wurmbrand continued by recalling the relationship of God and Moses in the Old Testament. In the Bible it is written that 'God spoke to Moses face to face' (Exodus 33:11). Wurmbrand, being of Jewish origin and fluent in Hebrew, explained the phrase 'face to face' is an old Hebraic expression meaning that God spoke to Moses 'as a person to a person'.*
>
> *'Suppose for an instant,' Wurmbrand explained, 'that Moses did not have a face. Suppose that Moses did not have a personality of his own. God could not have spoken to him anymore.'*

In Islam you are like a small cog in a big machine. It is not because I love God and He loves me, it is because I am following an order from God. We must obey our imams, our sheiks...

In Islam, nobody has a unique personality. If we want say somebody is good man in Islam, then they must be somebody with a position – a sheik or imam or leader in some way. It is not possible to say a normal person is a good person.

We don't have the idea that we talk to God and He talks to us. It is rude to do that. If you want to talk to God... read the Qu'ran. MAX

Moses was an individual and consequently was able to have an individual, personal relationship with God. God can no more have fellowship with us if we are not individuals than we can have a personal relationship with a stone.[1]

The post-modern friend I was talking with about God when coming back from a sailing trip said the main problem was that the Christians he knew didn't take responsibility for their actions. They were faceless individuals without character who waited for others to tell them what to believe. Almost that they were people too bound up in accountability to others. Our unthinking reliance on others to tell us what to believe; our unthinking repeating of what we perceive to be truth is an active inhibitor for people to hear about the Truth. The Truth is about a relationship, an individual relationship.

There is an evil inherent in both Communism and cults that renders them synonymous: they seek to destroy our individuality before God.[2]

I would add, from talking to some people who have decided to follow Jesus, that same issue is true in Islam. Islam seeks to have all men identical before God without any individuality in that relationship. The Good News we share is that God wants us to have this individual relationship, and it is because of this we have to be responsible for our sin.

The example Linda Berg uses, and I think it is probably the clearest example in the Bible, is that of David and Bathsheba. Because King David is a whole person with personality he made mistakes. He sinned. The most obvious one being the adultery with Bathsheba which then led to having her husband murdered.

He was confronted by Nathan the prophet about what he had done. David responded simply 'I have sinned.' He didn't try to make excuses or justify himself or explain it away. He stated without anything more, 'I have sinned against the Lord' (2 Samuel 12:13) He accepted it as an individual 'I' is the word he used. He accepted that even though Bathsheba was beautiful it was his lust that led him into sin. He accepted that he was responsible for his action.

Because of his acceptance of his sin he could, as an

There was a very famous imam in our town and he was talking with someone in the street. A friend of mine came across them in the street and saw them talking together. He knew both of them, that is he knew of the imam although he is not a friend and the other person he knew well.

The person who was talking to the imam said to the imam, 'Let me introduce you to my friend'. But the imam replied, 'It's not important for me to know him, but it's important for him to know me'.

This is the same in Islam between us and God - its not important for God to know us, but for us to know God. This is so different to the truth, that God sees us as precious in His eyes. MAX

1 Pp159-161 'The Children of God' by Deborah (Linda Berg) Davis
2 P 161 'The Children of God' by Deborah (Linda Berg) Davis

individual, turn to God and throw himself on His Grace. It was because of a personal relationship with God that he could do this. A faceless individual has no relationship.

With the media we are in transition. From one way to two way. We can trace the mass media back to Caxton and the printing press. Prior to Caxton, scribes hand copied books. Can you imagine hand-writing your own copy of the Bible? I think I would have chosen one Gospel and left it at that! But God called people through the ages to be scribes and copy the Scriptures so we have copies today.

When printing came about, a single book could be copied many thousands of millions of times and distributed. The modern publishing industry was born. Publishers determined what would and would not be published. When I wrote the first draft of this book in 2007 the next two paragraphs were these:

> *If this book is published it will be because a publisher has decided that either it has sufficient value to be published or that they will make enough money from the sale of the book. Either way, someone other than me would have decided to publish.*
>
> *Radio, TV and films work in broadly the same way. Someone somewhere decides that the content has sufficient value to duplicate or broadcast the message.*

Already, that has changed. This book is published through CreateSpace, which is a subsidiary of Amazon.com Inc. Through CreateSpace anyone can publish a book, DVD or CD. The system they use is called 'print-on-demand' or POD for short and allows them to produce a book, CD or DVD when the person orders it.

When the Internet first became available and we were using it back in 1992/1993, a friend of mine who publishes and writes was absolutely horrified. 'Who will act as the publisher and decide whether something has value or not?' was his legitimate question. What I liked about the burgeoning Internet was that the publisher gatekeeper was at last removed. Everyman is his own publisher. That was exactly what horrified my friend.

But still primarily it was a one-way street. Someone with a message passed it out to people who received that message. Christians have always been early adopters of new methods of communication in their desire to spread the Good News far

Is the Internet making people think differently? Fathers and mothers and older people don't use the Internet. They look at the Internet when their kids are doing it and don't understand.

The kids may find something out and then they may correct their fathers misconceptions. Schools now ask kids to use the Internet for research. But in general people like to play games or watch movies off the Internet, not for educating themselves.

People who can use a computer and can use the Internet tend to look down on people who don't. I am happy if I can use the Internet and my parents don't: 'Oh, they are simple people, they don't know what I do'. MAX

and wide. As radio and TV became widespread they realised a problem - if someone wanted to respond to the message, how could you help them? 'Follow up' ministries were developed. Initially responders wrote letters to the broadcasters, then teams of people read, prayed and wrote back. In the Middle East this could take many weeks for a response to a question to get back to the person asking.

Secular media were using phone-in shows as a way of interacting with their audience, but since a lot of the Christian broadcasting was international, this rarely happened in the Christian world.

With the Internet came email. Suddenly a letter could arrive by email within hours and more recently within seconds. But although the transport might be quick, if people were responding to a radio or TV programme the email would usually be written after the programme had finished and the response by the follow-up team within a few days.

Then came SMS or text messaging from our mobile phones. This was truly instant. Alongside this there were various instant messaging systems on the Internet. Still, primarily the thinking was inherited from letter follow-up, where the communication was only marginally influenced by the audience. Frequently programmes were prerecorded and so they could not be changed. It was still very much a one-way street.

This was also the picture when the Internet started to be used for sharing the Gospel. It started as a one-way source of information - text and images initially - with email as the only interaction. Today with what we call Web 2.0 we have such opportunities for interaction we are almost over run with them. From instant messaging through Skype and other voice technologies, with web TV, the ability to create content on other peoples websites and social networking sites.

The term 'broadcasting' was created to mean sending out a message that many could receive and see or hear. TV and radio were broadcasts. These media, because of their audience, needed to have a broad appeal. There was no space for niche programming. With cable connections [TV and radio] to our homes and satellite connections offering many thousands of channels the opportunity for narrow-casting arose. Narrow casting is where the audience is limited and the content specifically targeting a minority interest.

We have now moved into the era of inter-casting, where the audience could be large or small but it has the opportunity to interact with the content in real time.

Bill Gates in his book *The Road Ahead* said that we were facing a change in culture to what he called web lifestyle. When that happened he said, the change would be swift and irrevocable. We have passed that gateway now. Although we can go to shops, the price difference between ordering online and buying in a local shop suggests that at least for some goods, the days of the high street shop are numbered. I love browsing shops, and my family particularly like book shops, but we buy most of our books and DVDs online now. If it were available in our area, I suspect my wife would prefer to do our weekly shop online rather than at the supermarket.

This change to web lifestyle challenges personal relationships. About fourteen years ago I remember visiting a friend of my wife's in Chicago. They had developed their friendship over email and BBS forums. This was before the days of wide Internet accessibility. It was uncanny visiting this family. They knew all about us, down to details like how I preferred my cocoa. It was like we had lived next door for some years. Yet we had never met them before.

Though virtual relationships are possible, I still struggle with the need for incarnation within a relationship. God did after all make us whole people with bodies, minds and spirits and a relationship that leaves us with only two of those used is somewhat lacking. The same is true in our relationship with God. He is interested in us as whole people - body, mind and spirit.

Nailing jelly to a tree

From my experience it's difficult communicating our relationship with Jesus with other people. When we try to do that cross-culturally or to people from another world-view then the difficulty is multiplied. It's almost like trying to nail jelly to a tree – the phrase which President Theodore Roosevelt used to describe the seemingly impossible negotiations with Columbia when trying to dig the Panama canal.

The parallel of producing media to communicate the love of God to the people of the Middle East and digging the Panama Canal seems interesting. There were many aborted efforts in digging the canal. It cost an inordinate amount of money and life – at one point they were taking a trainload of dead every day away from the digging site. Yet when complete the canal short-circuited the route from the Atlantic to the Pacific oceans. So when we get the right media to communicate the love of God with Muslims – it might cost an inordinate amount of money and time - then it will significantly accelerate the process of sharing the Good News of the Messiah with the people Jesus came to die for.

When we look at what we and other media groups are doing, I often feel we are doing what's possible and not what's necessary. For instance, when a colleague left one country he wanted to give a gift of a short wave radio to each of the team members who had been involved in the production of programmes for a short wave station. Nowhere he looked could he find short wave radios to buy in that country. Young people all listen to FM radio there.

The traditional method using media to communicate the Gospel seems to yield very low results. For instance, one team we work with was involved in following up people who communicated with the TV station as a result of the programmes broadcast. They managed to meet about 50-60% of those who gave their name and address. 5% of them were prepared to talk and went through a course called 'Discovery' which shared the Gospel in a culturally relevant way. 1% of them accepted the Messiah as their Lord[1]. We cannot tell how many watched the programmes and didn't contact the station, if one in a thousand contact the station then 0.001%

It's very difficult and very hard... just one thing I want to ask Muslims... 'Are you honest in your love of God and are you ready to do anything to follow Him? Are you really ready to do anything to follow Him? Or are you just enjoying a shape – you like the shape of Islam and want to carry on.'

Also I feel myself that I cannot do it by myself. I must rely on God. I say to Him, 'God my heart is for this person to come to you, but I cannot do anything, you have to open His hear to you'. MAX

1 Figures from team working in the Middle East among the majority population

accept through this very expensive medium - in terms of cost and manpower.

For some people in the region Internet dialogue is almost addictive. One Arab study in 1999 interviewed 1000 users of the Internet from Saudi Arabia, Egypt and the Emirates. They found that the younger people, aged 14-24 were those primarily involved with online chat. I suspect that they have continued to use it as they have grown older so would now expect the primary age-group for online dialogue to be 14-30.

In that survey, some Saudi Arabian students admitted to spending more than 60 hours per week chatting online. Though some of the chat will be trivial and of no consequence, I do remember personally chatting online with a 22 year old student from Egypt. She was very open to hearing about the Messiah and many times I recounted to her the parables that He told as they were relevant to her situation as she shared with me. This involved both dialogue and storytelling.

The way ahead

When I was talking with my oldest son about the ministry he is working in, which is within a very different context to mine, he was telling me about the sort of event he would like to run: A sort of coffee bar, with music, drama, video clips, all asking rather than answering questions. At each table in the coffee bar would be a member of the team, primarily there to listen not preach. This is the start of dialogue, and allows the listener to think and engage with content.

I realised when he described this, it was exactly following the model that I am proposing in this book: to take a creative approach to communicating the gospel in a way that focuses on dialogue with a post-modern generation. Otherwise our 'evangelism' may well become an obstruction to people coming into loving relationship with God.

Jesus called a man-made obstruction a *skandalon* - something which prevents people coming to faith. One of his severest condemnations is directed at anyone who puts a barrier in front of 'one of these little ones': it would 'be better for you if a great millstone were hung round your neck and you were thrown into the sea'.[1]

I don't believe a creative dialogue to be anti-scriptural, from all I have read in the Bible it is very similar to the way

1 Emerging Evangelism - John Finney - page 126

Jesus communicated. Paul took communicating the Gospel to new depths when he spoke at Athens. He went on to say he wanted to be all things to all men for the sake of the Gospel. We need to re-capture that contextualisation.

But don't let us lose some of the blessings of modernism - let's evaluate and measure and bring before the Lord what we do. This is one of the paradoxes of faith of Charles Finney which has led evangelism astray for many decades not in his attempt to evaluate and measure, but in his exclusive use of that method to determine the content and style of his communication. We should follow the Lord's calling and use our God-given creativity not our effectiveness, but evaluation of what we do is only good stewardship of His resources.

In the *Walk Thru the New Testamant* they have a table to show that the 400 years of silence just prior to Jesus coming was in fact God preparing the way. The Greek, Israeli and Roman civilizations all contributed something to the Gospel's advance. The Greeks contributed a universal language, the Israelis a messianic hope and Rome a network of roads.

The universal trade language of Greek facilitated an ease of communication across three continents. The messianic hopes of the Israelis brought an expectation of the King and his Kingdom and the Roman roads gave efficiency of travel throughout the known world.

The seminar went on to challenge us to think of parallels in the 20th [and 21st] century. If we go back 400 years from today, we would see a world with few advances from the time in which Jesus walked this earth. Yet within the last two decades I have been on four continents and communicated through English. The motor car and more recently the jet aeroplane means within five hours we can be somewhere that would have taken months along Roman roads.

The Internet has meant that even flying seems slow in virtual travel terms. Those 400 years have brought us modernism with all these advances, and a hope for a better world, while rejecting on the whole the spiritual. Post-modernism has embraced all the technology and with it brought a hunger and thirst for the spiritual. There are indeed parallels today with the preparations God made for his son's arrival on earth.

'Start with the Church and mission will probably get lost. Start with the mission and it is likely the Church will be found.'[1] We need to re-find the creativity in mission that was

1 Mission-shaped Church - Church of England's Mission and Public Affairs Council - page 116

If I am talking to a Muslim I want to say, 'Please don't switch off your mind - follow your heart, but don't switch off your mind. Just come to God and say 'I cannot come to you without you helping me' but if you feel you can get to God in your own strength then you will never get to God.'

My two questions for anyone from the Middle East - Muslims or Christians - are these:

1. Do you really love God? Are you ready to follow Him wherever He leads you?

2. How can you get to God - either through your mind [logic] or through your heart [spirit]?

If you were converted though logic then someone coming along with better logic will change you to another religion. But if it is a relationship in your heart with the living God, though logic is important, the relationship with God will sustain you. Nobody can take you from God if you have a real relationship with Him.

MAX

there at the start of the church and in doing so, I believe the church will be re-found and our modernist communication will no longer be a stumbling block to pre-modern or post-modern Muslims.

If the church rediscovers creativity and re-enters into a dialogue approach to communicate the Gospel, this will be good news for me, and others like me, in re-finding our place in the body of Christ. It will be even better news for the average person from the Middle East who has, for different reasons, rejected our didactic and modernist approach into his world.

Bibliography

Seven Pillars of Wisdom by TE Lawrence
Published by Wordsworth Editions Ltd; New edition edition (1 Jun 1997)
ISBN-10: 1853264695
ISBN-13: 978-1853264696
Comment: Really excellent book to help understand Arabic worldview. The edition I have is much older than this, so not sure if the preface is the same.

Soul Survivor: How My Faith Survived the Church by Philip Yancey
Published by Hodder & Stoughton Religious; New edition (20 Nov 2003)
ISBN-10: 0340862297
ISBN-13: 978-0340862292
Comment: One of the books that helped me feel normal.

The Closest Thing To A White House Chaplain by Edward B. Fiske
Published by New York Times Magazine (8 January 1969)

1994 Christian Life and Witness Course video by Kel Richards, National Coordinator for BGEA Australia
See http://www.christianebooks.com/The_Billy_Graham_Formula_Graham.htm

Billy Graham - Personal Thoughts of a Public Man by David Frost
Published by Chariot Victor Publishing (August 1997)
ISBN-10: 0781415454
ISBN-13: 978-0781415453
Comment: The statistic of 25% 'success rate' for long term commitments is quoted by David Frost from his TV programme on PBS on 23 January 1993 'Reverend Billy Graham talking with David Frost'

Emerging Evangelism by John Finney
Published by Darton Longman & Todd (25 Oct 2004)
ISBN-10: 0232524963
ISBN-13: 978-0232524963
Comment: Excellent book for considering the emerging generation.

The Mathematical Theory of Communication by C.E. Shannon and Warren Weaver
Published by University of Illinois Press (Dec 1949)
ISBN-10: 0252725484
ISBN-13: 978-0252725487

What's Gone Wrong With the Harvest? A Communication Strategy for the Church and World Evangelization by James F. Engel
Published by Zondervan (Jun 1975)
ISBN-10: 0310241618
ISBN-13: 978-0310241614

Tell It Often, Tell It Well by Bill Bright and Mark McCloskey
Published by Here's Life Publishers, 1985

Good News Down the Street by Michael Wooderson
Published by Church Pastoral Aid Society (Dec 1987)
ISBN-10: 1897660200
ISBN-13: 978-1897660201
Published by Grove Books Ltd
ISBN-10: 1851742549
ISBN-13: 9781851742547

Saints Alive! by John Finney and Felicity Lawson
Published by Lynx Communications (1 April 1994)
ISBN-10: 0745931405
ISBN-13: 978-0745931401

Alpha Course Manual by Nicky Gumbel
Published by Alpha Publications (1 Jan 1999)
ISBN-10: 1898838003
ISBN-13: 978-1898838005

Why Worry? How to Live Without Fear and Worry by K Sri Dhammananda
Published by Buddhist Missionary Society (1996)
ASIN: B000YC8NYO
Comment: Good book to see insight into how Buddhists think

Mission Frontiers, September-October 2006
Are We Accelerating or Inhibiting Movements to Christ?
http://www.missionfrontiers.org/2006/05/contents.htm
Article - Are We Accelerating or Inhibiting Movements to Christ? by Bob Goldmann
http://www.missionfrontiers.org/2006/05/PDFs/08-13%20Explosive%20Kingdom%20Advance.pdf

Branded Nation: The Marketing of Megachurch, College Inc., and Museumworld by James B. Twitchell
Published by Simon & Schuster (August 23, 2005)
ISBN-10: 0743243471
ISBN-13: 978-0743243476

New York Times May 9th 2002
Megachurches as Minitowns by Patricia Leigh Brown

Operation World by Patrick Johnstone, Jason Mandryk and Robyn Johnstone
Published by Authentic Lifestyle; 21 edition (30 Sep 2001)
ISBN-10: 1850783578
ISBN-13: 978-1850783572
Comment: Gives a full list of the religious background to every country in the world. If you like statistics, you'll love this book!

Pagan Christianity: The Origins of Our Modern Church Practices by Frank A. Viola
Published by Present Testimony Ministry (May 2003)
ISBN-10: 0966665732
ISBN-13: 978-0966665734
Comment: This book will make you think. Some of his facts are wrong, but enough is right to make it a worthwhile read.

Walk thru the New Testament Seminar by Bruce H. Wilkinson
Published by Thomas Nelson (1982)
ASIN: B000J54EFS

The Courage to Create by Rollo May
Published by W W Norton & Co Ltd; New Ed edition (20 April 1994)
ISBN-10: 0393311066
ISBN-13: 978-0393311068
Comment: Very good book for thinking about creativity in communication.

Art at the Turn of the Millenium editors Burkhard Riemschneider Uta Grosenick
Published by Benedikt Taschen Verlag GMBH (1999)
ISBN-10: 3922873934
Comment: Interesting miscellany of art at the end of The 20th century, some shocking

The Complex Christ: Signs of Emergence in the Urban Church by Kester Brewin
Published by SPCK Publishing (20 Jul 2004)
ISBN-10: 0281056692
ISBN-13: 978-0281056699

Jumpers by Tom Stoppard
Published by Faber and Faber; 2Rev Ed edition (11 Aug 1986)
ISBN-10: 0571145698
ISBN-13: 978-0571145690
Published by Faber & Faber (1979)
ASIN: B0010VFELS
Comment: Probably one of the best plays ever written to communicate the paradox of God.

Bacon Sandwiches and Salvation: An A-Z of the Christian Life by Adrian Plass
Published by Authentic Lifestyle (9 Feb 2007)
ISBN-10: 1850787239
ISBN-13: 978-1850787235
Comment: Required reading to keep you sane.

What's So Amazing About Grace? by Philip Yancey
Published by Zondervan (Dec 1997)
ISBN-10: 0310218624
ISBN-13: 978-0310218623
Comment: Required reading when you don't feel sane.

Post-modern Youth Ministry by Tony Jones
Published by Zondervan/Youth Specialties (May 1, 2001)
ISBN-10: 031023817X
ISBN-13: 978-0310238171
Comment: Excellent book to help understand the current generation.

The Children of God: The Inside Story by Deborah Davis, Bill Davis
Published by Zondervan (May 1984)
ISBN-10: 0310278406
ISBN-13: 978-0310278405
Comment: Read the book and then think how of many sects, cults etc you know which display frightenly similar characteristics.

The Road Ahead by Bill Gates
Published by Viking (24 Nov 1995)
ISBN-10: 0670859133
ISBN-13: 978-0670859139

Mission-Shaped Church with foreword by Rowan Williams
Published by Church House Publishing (20 Jan 2004)
ISBN-10: 0715140132
ISBN-13: 978-0715140130

Made in the USA
Charleston, SC
23 February 2010